Dear Vic,
Dorothy

POLITICS and PONIES

Best reagard to our very
good friends –

Howard & Shannon

Other Books by Bill Heller

A Good Day Has No Rain: The Truth About How Nuclear Test Fallout Contaminated Upstate New York

Above It All: The Turbulent Life of Jose Santos

After the Finish Line: The Race to End Horse Slaughter in America

Billy Haughton: The Master

Captain Free-Lance: The Check Is in the Mail

Exotic Overlays: How to Get Big Payoffs from the Pick Six, the Pick Three, Exactas, Triples, Doubles and Superfectas

Go for the Green: Turf Racing Made Easy

Graveyard of Champions: Saratoga's Fallen Favorites

Harness Overlays: Beat the Favorite

Howard Parker: A Saratoga Harness Legend

Obsession: Bill Musselman's Relentless Quest to Beat the Best

Overlay, Overlay: How to Bet Horses Like a Pro

Playing Tall: The Ten Shortest Players in NBA History

Randy Romero's Remarkable Ride

Run Baby Run: What Every Owner, Breeder and Handicapper Should Know About Lasix in Racehorses

Saratoga Tales: Great Horses, Fearless Jockeys, Shocking Upsets and Incredible Blunders of America's Legendary Race Track

Stolen Lives: Albany High Class of '53, '54 ...

The Ten Commandments of Value

The Will to Win: Ron Turcotte's Ride to Glory

Thoroughbred Legends: Forego

Thoroughbred Legends: Go for Wand

Thoroughbred Legends: Personal Ensign

Travelin' Sam: America's Sports Ambassador

Turf Overlays: How to Handicap Grass Winners That You May Be Missing

POLITICS
and PONIES

THE FASCINATING LIFE OF
HOWARD NOLAN

BILL HELLER

ARCHWAY
PUBLISHING

Adapted and revised from the original manuscript by
Shannon L. Nolan for accuracy and clarity
Book production assisted by Benjamin Heller

Archway Publishing books may be ordered
through booksellers or by contacting:

Archway Publishing
1663 Liberty Drive
Bloomington, IN 47403
www.archwaypublishing.com
1 (888) 242-5904

ISBN: 978-1-4808-6387-3 (sc)
ISBN: 978-1-4808-6388-0 (hc)
ISBN: 978-1-4808-6386-6 (e)

Library of Congress Control Number: 2018950354

Print information available on the last page.

Archway Publishing rev. date: 08/15/2018

From Howard

To my sister, Mary Beth Collins, whom I adore, and who is the nicest person I have ever known; my parents, who gave me a lot of love, encouragement, and direction, and paid for my education; my lovely, supportive wife, Shannon; my children and grandchildren; and all the friends over the years who have made me the person I am today. I am truly blessed. Thanks to all of you.

From Bill

To Marianne, my love

ACKNOWLEDGMENTS

I have never had more fun interviewing a subject for a book. Howard was unwavering in his patience, cooperation, and time, and I'm honored to call him my friend.

My son, Benjamin, who assisted in putting the whole book together, and was a great source of encouragement.

My love, Marianne, didn't let two full knee replacements prevent her from helping me in so many ways. Most of all, she was her sweet, understanding self when I needed it most. I'm blessed to have her in my life.

Thanks to Howard's seven children and one grandchild for doing interviews. Also, thanks to Mary Beth and Mike Collins, Jim Tedisco, Marcia Aronowitz, Milt Aronowitz, Carl McCall, Victor Oberting, Joe Nolan, Bob Fierro, Peggy MacFarland, Justin Heller (who was especially helpful even though we're not related), Fred Martin, Tom Nolan, the Reverend Peter Young, Jerry Jennings, Bob Warsh, Ron Canestrari, John Hicks, Ed Reinfurt, Pat Palermo, Mike McNulty, and Neil Breslin. An extra thanks to Barbara Zwack, Joyce Roman, Larry King, Monique Koehler, Diana Pikulski, and Mike Hoblock. Thanks to Stephanie Barrell of the New York State Library and James Davies of the Albany Public Library.

A special shout-out to my dear friends Al and Sue Apicelli and John and Ann Durso.

To anyone I've missed, please forgive me.

CONTENTS

LIST OF IMAGES

Howard as an infant in 1932
Howard on pony Mickey, and his dad
Howard and his parents
Howard with his baby sister, Mary Beth
Mary and Kevin Langan (front), and Dorothy and Victor
    Oberting
Howard, Lee and Marcia Aronowitz, Rita and Bob Slocum
Mark and Carolyn Heller
Howard, Jim Mulcahy, and Norris MacFarland
Ruth Logan, Shannon's mom; sister Marcia; Shannon; and
    sisters Mary and Shasta (Credit Tom Brander)
The Nolan children (left to right): Anne, Debbie, Bob, Kathy,
    Karen, Lynn, and Donna
Howard's daughters (left to right): Lynn, Donna, Anne, Karen,
    Kathy, Howard and Debbie (front)
Howard and his son, Bob
Grandson Nolan Cummings and Howard
Howard and his sister, Mary Beth
Howard and lifelong friend Father Peter Young (Courtesy
    NYS Senate)
Albany Mayor Erastus Corning and Howard (Courtesy
    NYS Senate)
Margaret and Fred Martin and Howard

Howard's senate staff in later years (left to right): Dwayne
    Williams (intern), Barbara Jensen, Barbara Zwack
    Ardman, Nebraska Brace, Howard (front), Chris
    Gifford, Michael Flynn, Nona Teabout, Charlie Gaddy,
    and Pat McCarville. Missing Larry King (Credit NYS
    Senate)
Comptroller H. Carl McCall and Dr. Joyce Brown
Lt. Gov. MaryAnn Krupsak, Gov. Hugh Carey, and Howard
Sheriff Jack McNulty, Howard, Assemblyman Dick
    Conners, and US Rep. Mike McNulty (Courtesy NYS
    Senate)
The Wildensteins, Bailey, Fabre, and Nolans in the winner's
    circle in 1993 at the Breeders' Cup Classic
    (Credit Skip Dickstein)
Arcangues with Bailey and Fabre (Credit Shyeki Kikkawa)
Hy Rosen cartoon (Courtesy the Times Union)
Howard Nolan (cover) (Courtesy NYS Senate)
Howard and Shannon Nolan after the surprise win (Credit
    Kathy Nolan)
Courtesy Estate of Mark Heller (61)
Courtesy Estate of Howard C. Nolan, Sr. (58, 59)
Credit HMC Assocs. (61)
Courtesy Estate of Lee Aronowitz (132)
Credit Shannon L.Nolan (60, 62, 63, 64, 129, 130, 131)
Credit Ashley Hyde (author's portrait)

Chapter 1

POLITICS AND HORSES

When Howard Nolan was ten years old, his father advised him, "Never get involved in politics or horses." The advice was half-hearted. "Of course, my dad loved them both," Howard said, laughing. Worse yet, his father introduced him to both at an early age.

Shortly after Howard turned five, his dad, a traveling auditor for the state of New York, arranged for his son to lead the Labor Day parade in Skaneateles, a small village on one of the Finger Lakes. Young Howard would lead the parade on a pony that his dad had rented for him earlier that summer. So there was Howard, schmoozing the crowd and riding a pony, a harbinger of a life centered on politics and horses.

Howard fashioned his life around those two challenging endeavors and enjoyed success in each while also establishing a vibrant law firm and prospering in real estate. "Every day when I wake up, I thank the guy upstairs," said Howard, now eighty-five. "I've been blessed with good health and a good mind."

Born at Albany Medical Center in Albany, New York, on August 24, 1932, Howard lived in Mechanicville, twenty miles north of Albany and ten miles south of Saratoga

Springs, until the family relocated to Albany when he was four years old.

His political success drew on the core values he learned while growing up—family, church, community, hard work, and public service. He was able to weave this tapestry from a genuine concern for others' well-being and by treating all people the same.

"I think that's why he was so popular," said his daughter Debbie Nolan Murray. "He returned phone calls. He found jobs for people. He gave 110 percent because he wanted to help them. He carried that into our home. Be grateful for what you have, and treat everybody the same. Everybody is the same on this earth. We're all going through difficult journeys, but we're always the same. I felt that my dad was in politics for the right reason—to help other people."

The Reverend Peter Young, a lifelong friend of Howard's, has spent most of his life helping people in Albany with alcohol and drug abuse problems. He said of Howard and himself, "Mother, father, family, school. We had the same principles, the way we looked at things, founded in strong traditions from Mom and Pop. You're not supposed to do anything wrong."

Carl McCall was a close personal and political friend of Howard. An ordained minister in the United Church of Christ and the first African American elected to a statewide position when he became the New York State comptroller in 1994, McCall said of Howard, "He works hard. He's driven. He's good with people because he cares about people. He really cares. He really takes his faith seriously. I do, too. Faith is important in terms of doing it and living it. That's what I think is the most important characteristic of Howard."

But as important as his Catholic faith is, Howard didn't hesitate to go to bat for his younger sister, Mary Beth, his only sibling, when she was a senior at Holy Names Academy and being pressured to become a nun. "I already had my uniform," she said. "He went down and had it out with the Mother Superior. He told them they put too much pressure on me, and to knock it off, and that it wasn't going to happen. It didn't happen. I came to my senses. I had been dating Mike Collins, whom I later married, and I wanted children, so it wasn't for me."

After graduating from Christian Brothers Academy in 1950, Holy Cross College in 1954, and Albany Law School in 1957, Howard served in the US Marines for three years in the judge advocate general's office and earned the rank of first lieutenant.

Back in Albany, he began his law career, eventually opening the highly successful law firm of Nolan and Heller with his lifelong friend and confidant Mark Heller. Mark's dad, Julius, was a highly respected reporter for the *Knickerbocker News*. (These Hellers are not related to the author.)

Howard's appetite for politics, whetted when he worked on John F. Kennedy's successful run for the US Senate in Massachusetts in 1952, was jump-started a dozen years later when he took a major role in Robert F. Kennedy's successful campaign for the US Senate in New York. Coincidentally, Howard, a talented athlete, had played football at Holy Cross against Harvard's Ted Kennedy, younger brother of Jack and Bobby Kennedy.

Still, Howard didn't run for political office until 1974, when he was surprised to be tapped to run as a senatorial candidate in New York's Forty-Second District, representing Albany and Greene Counties. Howard won that election and nine subsequent ones for the state senate. His only loss in an election came in 1977, when he had the nerve to challenge Albany mayor Erastus Corning in the Democratic primary.

When he faced Howard in that primary, Corning was in the midst of a record-setting forty-two years as mayor—longer than any other mayor of a major city in American history, including Richard Daley in Chicago. It was the only time another Democrat had the audacity to challenge the mayor, who was backed by a powerful Democratic machine run by Dan O'Connell—a political machine that rivaled New York City's Tammany Hall and Boss Tweed. Corning died in office at the age of seventy-three in 1982.

Howard, who had honored his promise not to challenge Corning while O'Connell was alive, declared his candidacy for mayor shortly after O'Connell died at the age of ninety-one in 1977. Howard was Albany's Man of La Mancha, daring to take on the unbeatable foe in Corning. "That was a first," said Jerry Jennings, who had his own long run as mayor of Albany from 1994 to 2013. "That was really large. It took a lot of guts to do that, especially in those days."

Despite a poll by the *Albany Times Union* that said he was ahead, Howard was crushed by Corning, nearly two-to-one. Though obviously disappointed, he resumed his tenure with the New York State Senate, winning term after term easily while he continued to grow his law firm and real estate interests.

Due diligence was an important part of Howard's success. One of his grandsons, twenty-two-year-old Joe Nolan, followed his grandfather to Holy Cross and is now working for Franklin Templeton Investments in New York City. Asked how he would describe his grandfather, Nolan said, "In one word, it would be *hardworking*. He's eighty-five, and he still goes into the office. He's always working. He's willing to outwork people. He said the key to being successful was to out-prepare them. When he was just beginning to work as an attorney, he worked for the City of Albany and won two municipal annexation cases against the Town of Bethlehem. He won versus high-priced lawyers. He always brings that up to me."

Howard may not fully realize the influence he's had on other people. Former US congressman Mike McNulty—whose dad, Sheriff Jack McNulty, was one of Howard's strongest supporters—said, "Howard gave me a piece of advice I've always remembered, something he learned in the marines. 'Remember the seven Ps: proper prior planning prevents piss poor performance.' In other words, do your homework."

Howard did his homework religiously, as reflected in his 10-0 record running for state senator. "Labor loved him," said Larry King, who served as Howard's close adviser. "It was hard for a Democrat to get anything through the senate, but he would try. If you needed something, he was always there. We created more than four thousand jobs."

While cultivating his successful dual careers as senator and lawyer, Howard raised his seven children—six daughters and one son—with his first wife, Geraldine "Gerrie" Leonard. Howard was separated from Gerrie for more than a decade before they divorced. By then, he had had the good fortune of connecting with Shannon Logan, then a purser in charge of stewardesses for Pan Am. They met in 1985 and married in 1988, a year after his divorce from Gerrie became final.

Shannon has been Howard's confidante, companion, and loving partner ever since. Simply put, they are great together. Pat Palermo, Shannon's friend and another former Pan Am purser, said it beautifully: "She just melted into his life, and she was happy to do so. It really, really worked out well."

There was great irony in Shannon and Howard's union. Her dad, Clayton Logan, had been elected mayor of Lakeland, Florida, in 1951, but then lost in a bid for the state senate.

Howard was elected a New York State senator ten times, but he lost in a mayoral primary to Erastus Corning.

A century earlier, Albany had elected a Mayor Nolan, though he was unrelated to Howard. Michael Nicholas Nolan had emigrated from Ireland to the United States in 1843 at the age of ten. He wound up in Albany, where he studied law. Then he moved to San Francisco, where he worked on the street railway system, quickly becoming manager. Later Nolan returned to Albany and became a partner in Beverwyck Brewing, a director of the National Savings Bank, and Albany's fire commissioner from 1869 to 1878. Running as a Democrat, he was elected mayor of Albany in May 1878. Then he was elected to the US House of Representatives for a two-year term from 1881 through 1883.

Here's the kicker: Michael Nolan also owned horses, including a champion steeplechaser, Burke Cockran, who was named for US Congressman Burke Cockran. When Howard found a painting of the horse in a bar/restaurant called L'Auberge des Fougere in Albany, he bought it and hung it in his law office.

After Howard retired from the senate in 1994 and his law firm in 1997, he turned more attention to his Thoroughbreds. As a state senator, Howard had been barred from racing Thoroughbreds in New York. Now, twenty-four years after retiring from politics, he is still breeding winners, including the filly Another Genius (daughter of Einstein), who began her career with victories at Saratoga and Belmont in 2016. Howard was president of the New York State Thoroughbred Breeders from 1998 to 2002.

Howard made a unique contribution to the racing industry, creating a program that matched retired and rescued Thoroughbreds with prison inmates ready to learn how to care for them. Started in New York in 1984, the program has been replicated in eight other states.

His greatest thrill in racing came in 1993 when he and Shannon bought a small share in Arcangues, a French horse who was scheduled to stand stud the following year. Before that, the horse's connections had entered him in the 1993 $3 million Breeders' Cup Classic at Santa Anita Race Course in California. Though Arcangues had never raced on dirt and went off at odds of 133–1 under future Hall of Fame jockey Jerry Bailey, he won by two lengths. He remains the highest-priced winner in the Breeders' Cup thirty-four-year history.

Howard's contributions to his community included decades of service to the Cerebral Palsy Center for the Disabled Foundation, culminating in chairing the board of directors, and serving on the board of directors at St. Peter's Hospital.

A lifelong Democrat, Howard nevertheless had many close friends and family members, including his sister, who are Republicans. "It made for interesting family get-togethers," said his daughter Kathy, chuckling. Back then, Howard, his family, and his friends lived in a universe far removed from the burlesque of the 2016 presidential election and the ongoing political divide threatening to take down the country in 2017. To this day, Howard still believes that all people, even if they are family or friends, can disagree on issues and still respect other points of view.

Mike Hoblock, a Republican, became a member of the New York State Assembly in 1978, just four years after Howard joined the senate. He then served as Albany County executive and won Howard's senate seat after Howard retired. "Howard's a great guy," said Hoblock, who has remained friends with Howard ever since. "I met him the first day I was in the assembly. He became a very good friend of mine even though we are from different political parties. It doesn't seem to be a big matter to us. We represented the same county [Albany], and we would work together. We were both in the minorities in our houses, but despite that, we got some things done."

As Howard explains, "In politics, I learned to do what you said you were going to do, and to cooperate with those whose opinions you don't necessarily agree with, in order to get things done for the good of all." Imagine that. Howard calls Hoblock "one of the best public officials I've ever met. There are plenty of good public officials on both sides."

Howard never imposed his lifelong affiliation with the Democratic Party on his children. As his daughter Lynn said, "He told us, 'I'm a Democrat, but you vote for who you want. Don't vote down the Democratic line.' You've got to admire that."

Howard has many admirers.

"He was a perfect politician, in the respect that he was what you would expect a public servant to be. We don't have too many of them anymore," said Bob Fierro, a biomechanical consultant on Thoroughbreds and, like Howard, a former president of the New York Thoroughbred Breeders. "He only wanted to do his job. He's a very, very unique individual."

Howard's brother-in-law, Mike Collins, knows. "I saw him in a variety of venues, and I was impressed with his genuineness and care. I'm a staunch Republican and he's a Democrat. He'd say, 'Okay, let's get another glass of wine and talk more.' He didn't hold grudges, which was amazing with all the negative stuff about politics. He'd try to get their kids a job. He really amazed me. I don't think I could be as forgiving as he was. I'm still amazed by that today. He's the real deal."

Howard is still going nearly full speed in his mid-eighties, though he's endured multiple medical problems over the past few years, including a triple bypass, prostate cancer, an aneurysm on his aorta, and skin cancer. None of that has prevented him from flying all over the country and internationally with Shannon and working far too many hours every week on his shopping plazas and horses.

"Over the years, I've asked him, 'Can you slow down a bit?'" Kathy said. She knew how he would answer. "That's not him. He wouldn't be who he is. I think it would kill him. He keeps on ticking."

Chapter 2

GETTING STARTED

On the day before Howard was born, August 23, 1932, War Hero—Man O' War's son—had captured the Travers Stakes at Saratoga Race Course thirty miles away. Howard missed that 1932 Travers, but he wouldn't miss many others, spending endless summers at the historic Saratoga Springs venue.

Howard's grandfather Thomas had been a bridge inspector for the New York Central Railroad. While he was inspecting a bridge near Saratoga Springs, the bridge collapsed. Thomas Nolan couldn't swim. "They found him a few hours later downstream a couple of miles," Howard said. Howard's dad, Howard Sr., the youngest of four children, was only two years old when he lost his father. Howard's paternal grandmother, who also died before he was born, was hard-pressed to provide for her four children. "My grandmother had to work hard," Howard said. "She did washing, menial things to keep her family together."

Howard's aunt Beatrice had a lengthy career as a city clerk in Mechanicville. His uncle Thomas, nicknamed "Bunny," became the largest plumbing contractor in Saratoga County. Helen, Howard's younger aunt, was a secretary at General Electric in Schenectady.

Howard's first cousin Dan, one of Thomas's three sons, was on the Mechanicville High School basketball team, which came to be known as "The Whiz Kids" when they built a record of 39–1. Even better at football, Dan became a Little All-American quarterback at Lehigh. Drafted in the third round by the Washington Redskins, he was traded before his first season to the Pittsburgh Steelers, where he played behind Bobby Layne and Lenny Dawson.

Tom, Dan's older brother, became a sales manager for Amoco in New England. And the third brother, Jasper, was a gifted athlete who earned a football scholarship to the University of Nebraska before a badly broken wrist ended his career. When Nebraska rescinded his athletic scholarship, Jasper transferred to Iona College. He became a schoolteacher and a force in the Republican Party, serving as the Republican county chairman in Saratoga Springs for twenty years before retiring in 2014.

Howard's dad quit school after the eighth grade at Mechanicville and played professional basketball in Troy. "He was supposed to be in high school," Howard said. Howard Sr. hadn't abandoned education, but rather had delayed it. He went to school at night, earning a high school diploma, and then went nights to Albany Business College. Eventually Howard Sr. had a forty-year tenure with the state of New York, mostly in audit and control. "He was a very interesting man," Howard said.

Howard's dad was also highly political, as was Ray O'Sullivan, Howard's great-uncle. O'Sullivan, a graduate of Fordham University, worked for the *New York Sun,* and covered city hall. He became friends with one of the leaders of Tammany Hall, John Curry, and was persuaded to work for Tammany Hall as secretary. "That meant he ran Tammany Hall," Howard said. "He spent forty years as secretary. They were the kings, the most powerful political force in the United States. That was when Al Smith became governor of New York, Jimmy Walker became mayor, Herbert Lehman became a US senator, and James Farley became postmaster general under FDR [Franklin Delano Roosevelt]. Ray used to come to Albany and have dinner at our house. He was a great storyteller, which was one of the reasons I became interested in politics, even in grammar school."

Howard continued, "My father was a very liberal Democrat by persuasion. He told me before he died that he had voted for two Republicans in his whole life. The first was Wendell Willkie in 1940, because he [Howard's father] didn't think anybody, including FDR, should be president for more than two terms. The other Republican was the son of a friend who ran for the New York State Senate. He confided all that to me before he died in St. Peter's Hospital after his second heart attack. It was absolution. I wasn't really surprised, because all his political friends were Democrats. He grew up in a family that was hard-pressed financially. He believed in the little guy."

Howard did, too.

"We really have a lot of politics ingrained in our souls," Howard said. And horse racing too, another thing for which he can thank his dad. "He loved it, but as a fan," he said.

Howard's father worked with the public service commission for two years before joining the state comptroller's office, eventually serving as director of auditing systems. "For several years, the state comptroller's office had to audit every community," Howard said. "He went around the state. He traveled a lot during those years. He was a traveling auditor."

Every summer, his dad would arrange his schedule so that he could do the books of a community near a lake. When Howard was five years old, his family spent the summer, from July through Labor Day, at Skaneateles, a small village on Skaneateles Lake, one of central New York State's Finger Lakes. "We rented a house, a nice colonial house, and there was a garage in the back that they used as a stall," Howard said.

Howard's dad rented a pony named Mickey for his son. "He just decided he wanted to surprise me," Howard said. "He put me on the back of the pony that night. Then I rode him every day that summer, usually at night when Dad came home." One evening, Howard lost the reins and fell. "Dad told me not to go fast again," he said. "I was bruised a bit, that's all. He put me back on the pony that night. I never was scared, for whatever reason."

News of Howard's riding acumen had spread in the small village of some fifteen hundred. The annual Labor Day parade was coming. "They called my father and asked if I could ride the pony to lead the parade," Howard said. "They thought it was nice to have a pony lead the parade." Howard needed no encouragement. "I was waving to people. For a five-year-old, it was a thrill."

Years later, Howard's sister Mary Beth laughed when she saw the picture of Howard on the pony in the parade. "This was the beginning of my brother's political career," she said.

Chapter 3

FRIENDS FOR LIFE

In Mechanicville, Howard lived in a two-story family house on Park Avenue, in a working-class neighborhood right by a park. His uncle Thomas, a plumber, owned the building. Howard and his family lived on the top floor, and Thomas's family, including Howard's cousin Tom, lived on the first floor. Tom was only a month older than Howard, and the two boys became very close, playing soldiers and cowboys and Indians. "I had quite a collection of soldiers," Howard said.

A year later, Tom and Howard noticed a can of red paint left outside the gray house next door. "We started painting the house. We were painting partners," Tom said.

"We decided we were painters," added Howard, "but our parents weren't too happy with it."

Neither were the people who lived in the house that they painted. "My dad gave them a free faucet outdoors to make up for it. It's hilarious now," Tom said. Howard's punishment was a week without his father's homemade ice cream.

When Howard was four, his dad decided to move the family to be closer to his office in the state comptroller's office, which was in the Alfred E. Smith Building in downtown Albany. Remarkably, though his job as an auditor required extensive traveling, Howard's dad didn't purchase an automobile until 1948, using the train for out-of-town jobs.

"During the war [World War II], we couldn't buy a car," Howard said. "They used car factories to make tanks and other vehicles for the military. Essentially, they stopped manufacturing automobiles for the public. Then after the war, everyone wanted one."

Howard's dad decided to build a house at 40 Buckingham Drive, on the corner of Colonial Avenue in Albany's rapidly growing New Scotland Avenue neighborhood. "The neighborhood was all new houses being built," Howard said. "We moved in during the summer."

His new home was a two-story, colonial-style with three bedrooms, all on the second floor. The bedroom at the top of the stairs would belong to Mary Beth, Howard's younger sister. A few steps on the left led to the other two bedrooms, one for Howard and one for his parents. On the first floor were the living room, dining room, kitchen, and a half bath. The attached garage, lacking a car, sat empty for many years.

Howard's home was within walking distance of the two elementary schools he'd attend, first St. Theresa's and then Public School 19. When Howard was in the fourth grade, St. Theresa's had become so overcrowded that several students had to stand during classes on a rotating basis. When Howard's mom visited the classroom, she was so appalled that she yanked him out of that school and sent him to PS 19, where he stayed through the eighth grade.

Outside of school, Howard—most kids called him Howie, How, or just H—enjoyed nearby Buckingham Pond. "I played hockey there all the time when I was a kid and early in high school. I was a pretty good hockey player. We played on Saturdays and Sundays. Kids from all round the city would come. There were always a lot of kids skating there, playing

15

hockey or figure skating. It was a different world. Kids didn't have cars. One of the things that was favored among young males was athletics. It was a lot of fun, and I was a fast skater."

When Howard learned that a new family with kids, the Hellers, had bought a house four doors away, he could hardly wait. "There weren't a lot of young kids in the neighborhood," he explained. "The day after they moved in, I walked down the street to meet my new neighbors."

Julius Heller, who became good friends with Howard's dad, was a highly respected reporter for the *Knickerbocker News*. His coverage of the courts earned him an award from the New York State Bar Association for the quality of his journalism. He also developed a freelance business as a photographer and served as the Albany city historian.

Howard knocked on the Hellers' front door and introduced himself to Mrs. Heller, who told him that her son, Mark, was in his room. Of course, not every ten-year-old is confident enough to knock on a new neighbor's door and introduce himself. "That was just me," Howard said. "I was a gregarious kid. I just was friendly. It always served me well in life. I attribute that to my mom and dad. They were great parents."

Howard went upstairs to meet Mark, who was one year younger than Howard. "I walked in the room and Mark was resting on pillows reading Jules Verne's *Twenty Thousand Leagues Under the Sea*," Howard said. "That's pretty impressive reading for a kid. Other kids were reading comic books. That was the beginning of a lifelong friendship. We became fast friends when I was in the fourth grade."

Mark also became Howard's long-term partner in their law firm and in real estate. "We never had a serious argument as partners, and that's very unusual in law," Howard said. "Mark was truly a genius, absolutely brilliant. He scored 100 on his New York bar exam. And a good guy, an exceptionally outstanding man. He was talented. He learned several languages and played the banjo. He was just an incredible human being."

Howard was no slouch in the classroom, graduating from high school when he was sixteen. "My mom thought I was a boy genius, but she was wrong," said Howard with a laugh. "Mark was a genius. I was a good student."

Howard had a good point. Though he was doing great in every other subject, he got an F in algebra for the first three of four marking periods. He told his mom and dad that his teacher was incredibly boring and put him to sleep, so his parents hired a tutor—and Howard posted a 93 on the algebra Regents Test.

Howard's mom, Helen Burke, taught in grammar school before Howard was born. "My mother had several siblings [one brother and two sisters]," Mary Beth said. "When my mom's father died in the bridge accident, it was hard to put food on the table. My grandmother sent my mother to Oswego to live with my mother's aunt, Mary 'May' Elizabeth, and her husband, John Vowinkel." Mary Beth, Howard's sister, is named for her great-aunt.

John "Rip" Vowinkel lived his entire life in Oswego, dying at the age of eighty-one. In 1905, Rip had pitched six games for the Cincinnati Reds, compiling a 3–3 record with four complete games and an earned run average of 4.17. At the age of twenty, he had been the third-youngest player in the National League. The rest of his baseball career was spent with the New London Whalers in the Connecticut State League (1903), the Utica Pent-Ups in the New York State League (1903–06), and the Buffalo Bisons in the Eastern League (1906–10). Rip batted and pitched right-handed.

Outside of baseball, Rip was the Oswego County coroner,

a manufacturer of patent medicines, a member of the Oswego County Highway Department, and the owner and operator of The Chocolate Shop. Rip's obituary claimed that he was the only man to ever pitch a no-hitter, bowl a 300 game, and shoot a hole-in-one in golf, but the obit admitted that those claims lacked documentation. "He was a very, very nice man," Howard said.

Because she lived in Oswego, Howard's mom got to attend college—quite an accomplishment for a woman in those days. "She was very fortunate," Mary Beth said. "My mom was able to go to college and graduate with a teacher's degree. When people read this in her obituary, they were shocked."

After Howard turned twenty-one, his mom returned to teaching as a substitute. "Then she had the opportunity to teach full-time," Howard said, "and she did so despite my father's disapproval." That was an act of courage on her part. "My father was a great guy, a best friend [to me] later. But [when I was] growing up, he was a tough taskmaster. I was up at seven thirty on Saturday mornings doing chores when all the other kids were sleeping. He was the disciplinarian in the family. Later in life, I learned the lesson of hard work. He instilled that in me. That was a great lesson to learn."

Howard credits his dad with teaching him many lessons. "My dad was an inveterate reader, especially interested in government. He just had a real interest in public life. He used to talk at the dinner table about government. He had a strong influence on me."

Thanks to his dad, Howard became a daily newspaper reader at a young age. "My dad read the *New York Times* cover to cover every day. I started reading it daily in grammar school." Howard not only read the news, but also delivered it. "I had a paper route, and back then, you had to collect the money. I got to know everyone's name and learned to appreciate the value of a dollar."

Howard's mom taught him to play bridge, Parcheesi, and Monopoly. "I actually became a pretty good bridge player," he said. "And I have never lost at Monopoly."

When Howard was nine, he was playing war games with a couple of his buddies in his bedroom on a Sunday morning. They had the radio on and heard about the attack on Pearl Harbor. "I'll never forget it," Howard said. He ran downstairs to tell his parents, who had not been listening to the radio.

Howard became an older brother at the age of seven, and he was to have a strong influence on his only sibling, Mary Beth. "My sister is a wonderful person. I've never had a cross word with her. She was class president during her last three years in college at St. Rose. She was a better student than I was. She's very outgoing, friendly, smart, and a great human being. She and her husband, Mike, raised five really nice kids."

Mary Beth idolized her brother, who was a strong male influence, especially since their dad frequently traveled out of town. "When we were growing up, it was just the two of us," she said. "Howard took me everywhere in the summer. We'd go to Crooked Lake, about an hour from Albany. He'd take his little sister along. I was about nine. We just had a very good relationship. We lived in a great neighborhood where we made lifelong friends. I was one of the youngest, but I was allowed to play. There were children playing hide-and-seek and kickball and kick the can. Everyone was included. It was a simpler time. You can't do a lot of those things now."

Then she added, "My big brother will always be a hero of mine. He's always been my idol. The day I turned sixteen, I got my driver's permit. Howard taught me how to drive. He did so well that I passed the first time."

Mary Beth got used to Howard doing well in just about everything he tried. "Whenever he was involved in something, he wanted to be the best he could be, no matter what it was, sports or a summer job. He was always self-assured, very active, very busy. When Howard went to law school and I went to the Academy of Holy Names on Madison Avenue, we would walk together every morning at six thirty to the church on New Scotland Avenue. We're both devout Catholics."

They are no longer both Democrats, however. "I changed many years ago," Mary said. "I didn't leave the Democratic Party—the Democratic Party left me. I'm a conservative Republican."

That did not affect their close relationship. "Howard told me of the error of my ways," said Mary, laughing. "I was very diplomatic about it. Howard told me that my father was spinning in his grave because I was a Republican. I just smiled. We just disagreed."

But politics did complicate Mary Beth's relationship with her boyfriend, Mike Collins, who was a conservative Republican. "Howard and I grew up in politics," Mary Beth said. "We were both Albany Democrats. I remember when I was dating my [future] husband, JFK was running for president and my boyfriend was a conservative. He [Mike] came to the door and my father was a big Democrat. My father opened the door a little bit and asked him who he voted for. Mike gave the right answer and he let him in."

Another time, Mike, who taught history at South Colonie for thirty-four years and at his alma mater, Christian Brothers Academy, for thirteen more, was with Howard when he had to stop at Dan O'Connell's home. Mike couldn't have been more nervous walking into the home of the head of the Albany Democratic Party machine. "I may have been the first

Republican in there," he said. "I figured they'd find out I was a Republican and I'd never get out alive." He did, though. "I still kid around with Howard about that," Mike said.

When Mike and Mary Beth began dating, Howard, who was in his senior year of law school, was an assistant football coach at Christian Brothers Academy. But Mike didn't know that when he first met Howard. "I was watching football practice, and Howard came over with Coach Bob Foster," Mike said. "I didn't know the assistant coach was my girl-friend's brother. It was a little bit embarrassing. I didn't recognize him at first."

Mike got to know Howard very well after that. "We played golf at Albany Municipal one day, and he made a hundred-foot birdie to win on the seventeenth hole, which annoyed the heck out of me," Mike said. "I'm probably exaggerating, but it was a very long putt. I'm very competitive. Howard is very competitive, too, but I didn't know it at the time. He wanted to beat that young whippersnapper. I'm seven years younger."

Although Mike always wanted to beat Howard on the golf course, he wanted to kill him one hot summer afternoon. They were fixing up an apartment house they had purchased, and Mike decided to tar the roof. Howard held the ladder so Mike could climb to the roof with his tools. "It was Saturday in late July," Mike said. "That meant cutting into his Saratoga time. So we got this big old wooden ladder, and I was tarring the roof. Howard yells up, 'Mike, I'll be right back.' I tarred for about an hour. When I was done, I wanted to carry my tools with me down the ladder, so I needed Howard to hold the ladder. It was getting hotter, I was baking, and Howard was nowhere to be found. An hour later, he comes strolling along carrying the *[Daily] Racing Form*. He yells, 'Mike, I forgot you were on the roof.' He had been at OTB [off-track betting]."

Mike should have been happy that Howard only went to a nearby OTB parlor. If he'd driven to Saratoga Race Course, he wouldn't have come back at all.

Mike has seen Howard in action at Saratoga. "He knew the valet's name," Mike said. "The guy selling the programs. He knows their families. How are their kids doing? The binocular renter. The usher. The waitress. He knew them, and they knew him, and they were genuinely friendly with him. They really liked him. What a good man he is."

Howard altered the direction of his sister's life, interceding on Mary Beth's behalf when she was being pressured into becoming a nun. "Father Edgar Holden told me that if I didn't go into the convent, I'd never be happy in life," Mary Beth said. "He was very wrong. I've had a wonderful life with five great children and eight grandchildren."

When Howard was eleven, he went with Mark Heller, Tom Spath, Ron Roberts, and the Neville twins, Peter and George, to see Albany mayor Erastus Corning and ask him to build a baseball diamond in their neighborhood. Corning would speak to each and every visitor who came to city hall to see him during his four-decade-plus tenure.

"Julius Heller set up the meeting with the mayor," Howard said. "Because he was the Albany city historian, he had great access to Erastus. My father and Julius were very friendly. Many a day, Julius would give my father a ride to work. They would drop off Mark at Albany Academy and go downtown. He'd drop my father off at the Alfred E. Smith Building and go to the *Knick News*, which was downtown then."

The erstwhile ballplayers needed a spokesman. "I was the spokesman," Howard said. "I was the ringleader in my neighborhood in sports. I was eleven. I told him we had a lot of kids in the neighborhood who liked to play baseball, and there was a vacant lot."

Corning made it happen in two months. "I was very impressed," Howard said. "We were awed by the mayor's power." The City of Albany contributed a backstop and laid out the diamond. Howard and his friends provided bags for bases. Thus was Howard's lengthy love/hate relationship with Corning born.

In a phone conversation three years ago, the *Times Union*'s Fred LeBrun—who was the newspaper's city editor, arts editor, and restaurant reviewer, and a greatly esteemed reporter and columnist—told Howard that deep down, Erastus liked him. "Corning was probably one of the four or five smartest people I've ever met," Howard said. "Very intelligent. He knew more municipal law than any lawyer I've ever met, and he wasn't even a lawyer. He'd quote statutes without looking, and when I'd check it out, he'd be dead-on every time. He was a very complicated man."

As a teenager, Howard also bumped into the mayor when he did groundwork and caddied at the former Albany Municipal Golf Course, not far from Howard's home. "We were low paid, but I met a lot of interesting people. That fanned my interest in politics and golf. That's where I learned to play golf. I wound up with a five handicap while I was in law school."

On a wintry day years earlier, Howard had met another lifelong friend, the Reverend Peter Young. "I think we met over a snowball fight," Young said. "I went to St. Theresa's, and he went to PS 19. The two grammar schools were a block apart. We had a lot of fun. We grew up together." Then they attended Christian Brothers Academy (CBA) together, though Young is two years older. Howard would be the youngest student in his class of 225 at CBA.

Young is still working nonstop in his eighties to help addicts. "I'll do that until I die," he said. "I know there's a mission. I've been doing it for sixty years, and I'm still trying to do the best I can every day."

Although Young may someday be designated a saint, he was just a normal teenage boy growing up with Howard. "We were always together playing, competing in the same sport," Young said. "Anything we could—basketball, baseball, football. We'd play golf for ten cents a hole. We were both competitive in every sport, and we've always been together. It was a fun time. He's an easy guy to get along with. It was a natural bonding."

Young wound up getting a baseball scholarship from Siena College in Loudonville, just north of Albany. "I played first base, where they put the fat guys," Young said with a laugh.

Howard's friendship with Young continues today, though there was one incident that almost killed it. "We were dating the same girls," Young said. "He got very upset with me one night. He was dating Ellen Morrissey while he was in college. I said, 'Howard, you're going back to Holy Cross tomorrow, right?' He said, 'Yes.' I said to Ellen, right in front of him, 'Can we go to the prom at Siena on Friday night?' And we did go to the dance. He was pretty mad at me."

Bob Warsh, whose store, Little Folks, was in Howard's Delaware Plaza just outside Albany, is another of Howard's longtime friends. "We lived on the same street and grew up together," Warsh said. "We hung around together. We didn't do anything different than other kids. We talked about sports. We played sports and we respected each other. That's the biggest thing of all. He dated my sister Anne for a couple of years."

Howard said of Anne, "She was drop-dead gorgeous."

Victor Oberting, who was born in Batesville, Indiana, and came with his family to Albany when he was eight, is another dear friend of Howard's, though they attended separate high schools. Howard went to CBA, while Oberting, who is three years younger, attended Vincentian Institute. "Only the wealthy kids went to CBA," Oberting said. "The smart kids went to VI. You had to be good-looking and smart to get into VI. He didn't qualify." When that observation was repeated to Howard, he couldn't stop laughing.

"We became close friends more than forty years ago when he was running for the senate," Oberting said. "I was doing fund raising for him. We belonged to the same club. We played golf together." Oberting, whose dad started the family's grain business, Interstate Commodities, in 1947, was a partner with Howard when he purchased Blue Sky Farm in 1977. "It was an interesting investment," Oberting said. "I got out after a few years. I lost a little bit on what I invested, but it wasn't a big amount. There were two hundred horses boarding there at one time."

Oberting's respect for Howard runs deep. "He was a gold standard in Albany because he was very honest. Howard was as honest as the day was long. He's very easy to talk to. He's the kind of guy you like to be with. He is one of my very best friends."

Howard and Mary Beth were delighted when their father's job took them to New York City. "My mom and I would go with them on the train," Mary Beth said. "They'd go to a ball game and we'd go to a Broadway show. I saw *South Pacific, Oklahoma,* and *Carousel.*"

Howard relished trips with his dad to see football and basketball games. "We saw Notre Dame play Army at Yankee Stadium three straight years when they were both great teams. I became a big Notre Dame fan. He also took me to see pro football games in Brooklyn [the Brooklyn Tigers] and New York Giants games at the Polo Grounds. I got to see Washington's Sammy Baugh, the best pure passer I've ever seen and a great punter. It was a different era. They called him Slinging Sam, the Redskin man. My dad took me to a lot of basketball games at the Garden. It took up a whole block. I was a very lucky kid. He loved sports."

Howard's dad was also a role model. "He didn't drink; he didn't smoke," Howard said. "That was also a plus. I didn't drink until I was in my thirties."

Howard was fourteen when his dad took him to Saratoga Race Course for the first time. He remembers that day as if it were yesterday. "They didn't run at Saratoga from 1942 to 1946 because of the war," he said. "It was 1946 when they ran for the first time in four years. I was hooked. I just loved it. I loved watching them run. They did have a much larger paddock than now.

"I saw a lot of great horses run, starting in 1946 when E. R. Bradley had a very fast two-year-old, Blue Border. He won the United States and Grand Union Hotel Stakes and the Hopeful. He broke records in two of the races. E. R. Bradley was one of the greatest horsemen of all time. Over the next few years I saw Rico Monte, Talon, and Gallorette, who was trained by El Gran Senor, Horatio Luro, a man I became very friendly with several years later." Luro, a legendary trainer, is forever remembered by his phrase about not overtraining Thoroughbreds: "Don't squeeze the lemon dry."

Not only did Howard attend all four Saturday cards at Saratoga Race Course, but he and his dad began doing doubleheaders those Saturday nights at Saratoga Harness, literally across the street. "I think every Saturday, my dad, after the races, he took me over to the harness track," Howard said. "I was doing doubleheaders." He laughed at the memory before continuing, "I really loved the flat track, but I got tired at night. It wound up that I had no interest in the Standardbreds." In contrast, his interest in Thoroughbreds has never wavered.

Chapter 4

SCHOOL DAYS

Long before Howard's name was in headlines about politics, he received recognition for his outstanding athletics career at Christian Brothers Academy. The private, Catholic, junior and senior high school for boys was founded in 1859 by the De La Salle Christian Brothers in Albany. Attending from ninth grade through a postgraduate year, Howard excelled in football, basketball, baseball, and track and field. He also skied and played golf in his free time.

As a 150-pound quarterback in his post-graduate year in 1949, he led the Brothers to a tie for the league title with La Salle. In the deciding game, the two schools played to a 20–20 tie, despite Howard's three touchdown passes. He was named All-Albany and All-Diocesan League. "Football was always my favorite sport," Howard said.

In track, Howard was a sprinter and a long jumper. "I was probably the fastest kid in Albany when I was at CBA," he said. He also pitched for the baseball team and then continued to play baseball for six years in the semi-pro Twilight League with the New York Centrals, all the way through Albany Law School. He would have played a seventh season, but while he was pitching in the season opener, he was struck in his right ear by a comeback liner. The injury required plastic surgery and would eventually leave him deaf in that ear, which helped Howard decide to concentrate on his final year in law school and give up baseball.

His absence on the CBA football field as a cocaptain in his senior season prompted a story by William Toomey in the October 30 issue of the *Knickerbocker News*. The headline read, "Injured CBA Grid Player Battles for Team on Sidelines." There was a three-column-wide picture of Howard, his right arm in a sling, in front of his teammates, who were all clad in CBA dress—collared shirt and pants. The story explained that Howard—also referred to as Howie—had broken his wrist while blocking for a teammate in a scrimmage before CBA's first game. Toomey quoted CBA Coach Pete Mooney saying of Howard, "He would have been one of the best in the city with a little experience."

Howard said in the story, "It is hard to realize that because of one unfortunate block in practice, I would no longer play football for CBA. Each time we'd make a sizable gain or hold the opposing team from a touchdown, I'd wish I were in there helping the boys. It is tough to see your team go on to victory without the feeling that you have helped them. Playing or not playing, it is still my team and I am with it all the way."

Toomey concluded his story by calling Howard "the type of youngster who has an abundance of school spirit and desires to have an active part in his school's achievements." Such was Howard's standing at CBA that he was chosen to speak to the student body in his senior year before the first game.

Twenty-six years later, Howard was asked again to speak to the student body at CBA on graduation day as a newly minted New York State senator. In a 1975 story in the *Knickerbocker News* by John LaRouche, Howard called the experience "one of the proudest moments of my life." Howard shared his belief of the importance of sports with LaRouche: "Athletics is great as far as developing a sense of participation. It teaches you how to get along with people and helps build character. As I look back, I can honestly say athletics played a big part in my development as a person."

After the speech, one of the students approached Howard and asked him if he would give some advice to young people who want to know the keys to being happy and successful. He had been asked a similar question before at another function, so he had given a good deal of thought to the subject--people looking for direction. After reflecting for a few minutes, Howard offered to share some of the principles he tries to live by:

1. Be honest.
2. Say what you mean and mean what you say. (i.e., have integrity).
3. Be adaptable. The only thing constant in life is change; if you don't change with the times, you will be left behind. Be open to new ideas and different approaches.
4. Be a good listener. You might learn something, especially from people who know you best. After all, you already know what you know.
5. Be sensitive to other people's feelings (i.e., have empathy and respect for others).
6. Work harder than your competitors. It's funny how the luckiest people seem to be the hardest workers. It's not always the most talented and the smartest who win. Oftentimes, it's the ones who try harder and are persistent. Improvement comes, not only from experience— of course— but from making mistakes. Constructive criticism is a gift to be cherished.
7. Don't be afraid to take informed risks. You make the best decisions with the most amount of information.

Be prepared for when a unique opportunity presents itself.

8. Do charity work without looking for recognition. As the quote is paraphrased, Bible (King James version); Luke 12:48 "To whom much is given, from him much is expected."

9. Have a positive attitude. You might not be able to control what happens to you, but you can control how you react to it. Where there's a will, there's a way.

10. Be true to yourself. Honor your instincts; they will help you avoid temptation.

11. Be a doer. Write down the things you want and need to do, and divide those goals into manageable tasks that you review frequently. Writing them down will make them happen, because it will feel like a commitment. Have a plan, and learn how to manage your time and money. Rome wasn't built in a day.

12. Be a communicator. Reach out to people. A thank you note or a phone call to compliment someone is always appreciated and only takes a few minutes. Little things do make a difference.

Howard also added that the happiest people he knows all have three things in common: 1) they are doing something that they are interested in (purpose); 2) they have good personal relationships (family and friends); and 3) they have control over their finances (security).

Howard still had a bit of development left at CBA. Because he was only sixteen, he was allowed a postgraduate year, and he played football for another season as the team's co-captain. At seventeen, he was still one of the youngest graduates that spring.

Howard continued his education at Holy Cross, a Roman Catholic, Jesuit college in Worcester, Massachusetts. "My father insisted I go to Holy Cross and that he would pay for it, partially because it was Catholic and a great school. I was offered football scholarships at Villanova, St. Bonaventure, Niagara, and Hamilton College, but not Holy Cross. It was funny."

The football coach at Holy Cross (1933–38, 1950–64) was Dr. Eddie Anderson, a consensus first-team All-American and team captain of the famed 1921 Notre Dame team, which was coached by legendary Knute Rockne. One of Anderson's teammates was George Gipp, subject of the famed "Win one for the Gipper" speech by Rockne. In his final three years at Notre Dame, Anderson's team went 28–1; the only loss was to the University of Iowa at 10–7. Anderson coached at Iowa from 1939 to 1942 and 1946 to 1949, with a four-year gap because of his World War II service with the US Army Medical Corps. Anderson was a gifted doctor who would work at the University of Iowa Hospital in the morning before coaching football in the afternoon.

Freshmen didn't play varsity football then, so Howard, who had grown to six feet and 160 pounds, played quarterback and safety for the Holy Cross freshman team. "I wasn't big, but I was good," he said. He missed the opener, a road game at Colgate, because of a bad cold, but then he played "a fair amount" against Dartmouth.

In the finale against previously undefeated Harvard, when Howard was matched against offensive/defensive end Ted Kennedy, he had a game of a lifetime in a 40–0 upset. "I had one of those games that anyone in sports would dream of," he said. "I threw one touchdown of forty yards and another [pass] for thirty to set up a TD. I ran for fifty-five yards for a TD and had a fifty-yard run to set up another."

Howard was invited to the five-week varsity spring practice as the projected second-string quarterback behind highly talented Charlie Malloy. It would be the only time Howard got to play for Dr. Anderson. "The man was an outstanding football coach," he said. "He was very meticulous and a very smart guy."

Howard played well enough at spring practice to be invited to join the varsity when practice began on September 1, but he never made it. He had asked Anderson for a scholarship, only to be told that there wasn't one available. "My father was paying the full boat, and he wasn't happy with my marks," he said. "He discouraged me from playing football." It made sense. Howard wasn't likely to improve his grades while playing football. So Howard, who figured he'd get little playing time behind Malloy anyway, turned his attention to baseball.

Both Howard, a pitcher, and Fred Martin, a new freshman friend and outfielder from Yonkers, wanted to play baseball for Holy Cross as sophomores. Their timing, however, wasn't great. "We were good high school players, but that was the year they went on to win the 1952 College World Series," Martin said. "We tried to make that team. It's funny." Neither made the team, but they developed a friendship that's lasted until today.

"Our friendship formed very quickly," Martin said. "We used to visit each other's homes." When Martin visited Howard's home in Albany, politics came up frequently. "I knew his father," Martin said. "His father and I used to fight over politics all the time. I was a rock-ribbed Republican, and he was a rock-ribbed Democrat. Howard and I have continued that all our lives. Lots of fun."

An accomplished attorney of more than fifty years with Bleakley/Platt, Martin has a background in horses. He's been the lawyer for Yonkers Raceway for decades, and he loved going to Saratoga Race Course with Howard in the summers. "We used to run down to Coulson's," Martin said. "We'd pick up the *Racing Form* around midnight and then handicap for a while in Howard's kitchen or at a local bar. Then we'd get into politics until three in the morning."

Martin said that in college, "We'd stay out of trouble. That's one of the good things. We were fairly serious students, but we had a lot of fun. We did a lot of traveling around New England. In the summertime, we'd return to Albany and Yonkers, respectively. Very soon, I would go up to Howard's house and stay a couple of weeks and go to Saratoga. I spent a lot of time at Lake George."

Martin did Howard an enormous favor, helping him land a job at Saratoga Race Course. "I actually helped Howard get a job with the people who ran the parking concession at Saratoga," Martin said. "My father happened to be their insurance agent. Howard was very proud of his job at Saratoga. He had already been an active participant at Saratoga for quite a time. When I would go up and visit him, he was very anxious to show me how many people he knew in the horse industry. We were up there for the Hopeful. Homer Pardue was a trainer who had a horse in a race. Howard goes over to him and says, 'Mr. Pardue, do you think your horse can run six and a half furlongs?' He said, 'Sure, son, if you give him enough time.'"

Another time at Saratoga, Howard and Martin were dating sisters. "We were taking the girls to the track," Martin said. "The father of the two girls, Dr. Wallingford, told us, 'Take my box.' That was one of our greatest days at Saratoga because we were strictly railbirds—no seats."

In 1966, Howard did Martin a favor. "I ran for Congress once," Martin said, "when I was thirty-two. Howard sneaked down to my fund-raising dinner. He said, 'Put me in the back of the room or the corner.'"

Forty years later, they would partner on a single Thoroughbred, Irish Colonial, perhaps the best horse—other than Arcangues—Howard ever owned.

Chapter 5

ONE OF A FEW GOOD MEN

In the summer of 1956, with one year left in law school, Howard was working two jobs, one for the City of Albany cutting grass at Albany Municipal Golf Course, the other on the graveyard shift, 11:00 p.m. to 7:00 a.m., at Allegheny Ludlum Steel. "My job was five nights a week, emptying silicon from railroad cars or dragging down steel bars from a furnace. It was hard work, but that served me well. I was used to hard work, and I was making good money."

When Howard graduated from Albany Law School in 1957, he was at a crossroads. He had gained valuable experience working that summer with Rosenstock and Turner, a law firm in downtown Albany. He wanted to continue his law career, but first he had to deal with his military obligation. "I had deferments in college and law school, but in those days, you had to serve in the military. I was young. I decided to join the military. I decided I wanted to be an officer."

Like he has done his whole life, Howard did his homework before enlisting. "I checked the army, navy, air force, and marines. I wanted to see which one had the lowest percentage of lawyers per thousand. I figured I'd learn more and have more to do. That's why I joined the Marine Corps. I laugh looking back, because obviously the Marine Corps had a reputation for making people toe the line." Howard, who would spend three years and three months of active duty in the marines and then six years in the active reserve, was no exception.

He spent the first eleven and a half months in the marines at Quantico, Virginia, thirty miles south of Washington, DC. "The first three months of camp were brutal," Howard said. "I had been drinking too much beer. I was 198 pounds as a senior in law school with a 37- to 38-inch waist."

The weight came off quickly. "The first two, three weeks I was miserable," Howard said. "We used to run twenty miles a day, and we did a series of four physical tests. I was down near the bottom in three of them—push-ups, pull-ups, and sit-ups. The other test was running a quarter of a mile. The second time I took the test, I improved. The final time, I finished first in three of the four—push-ups, sit-ups, and the quarter-mile run, in which I beat Riley Nixon, who had been captain of the track team at Virginia Military Institute. I went down to 172 pounds and my waist was 30¼ inches. I was so exhausted that I'd come home, go to dinner, go to bed, and get up at four in the morning."

Howard bought his first car, a 1937 Plymouth, in the spring of 1958 for fifty dollars from two brothers who were also his friends, Tom Jr. and Malcolm Magovern. Their dad, Tom, was the doctor at Saratoga Race Course. "Tom Jr. was in my class at Holy Cross," Howard said. "I spent seventy-five dollars fixing that car up and kept it for two years."

In January 1959, with help from his dad, Howard purchased a brand-new Chevrolet for $1,700. "I could afford it because my parents were very generous to me. They paid for my education. I had two weeks of leave, and my dad knew a Chevy dealer in Oneonta, about seventy miles from

Albany. We drove to Oneonta, my father and I, and I bought the Chevy."

Howard got leave to attend the December 1959 wedding of his friend Mike O'Brien in Albany. He drove his car to Washington, DC, parked, and took the train up to Albany. Traveling in uniform—and thereby receiving half off his train fare—Howard attended the wedding on Saturday and was on his way back to Camp Lejeune the next day.

When he arrived at the train station in Washington, DC, Howard noticed two women. "I saw these two attractive ladies struggling with their suitcases," he said. "They were kicking their bags forward." One was Gerrie Leonard, a junior at Trinity, a Catholic university for women in Washington. "I helped Gerrie with her bag," he said. "I had parked my car about a half mile from Trinity because it was free parking on the street. I hailed a cab, dropped Gerrie and her friend off at Trinity, and got my car."

After boot camp, Howard spent eight and a half months in Officer Candidates School in Quantico, where "you learn everything you need to about the Marine Corps. All marine officers do this," explained Howard. "Some became pilots; some became machine gunners. I became a lawyer in JAG, the Judge Advocate General's Corps."

Being at Quantico allowed Howard to spend most weekends in the nation's capital, thanks to his friend and Albany neighbor Tom Gallagher, who was attending Catholic University in Washington. "Tom lived kitty-corner from me in Albany and we were in the same class in law school," Howard said. "He had a roommate, Bob Piscarelli, and we met and went out to dinner. They had an extra bedroom at their apartment, and Tom insisted I spend weekends there. I took him up on the offer, got a key, and spent almost every weekend. I got to love Washington. It's a great city, with all the museums and restaurants."

And Gerrie ... Howard had gotten Gerrie's phone number when he gave her and her friend that cab ride from the train station. By coincidence, Howard had been invited to a prom at Trinity by June Griffin, another Albany neighbor and friend. Gerrie saw Howard at the prom and they began dating. "She was pretty, and she was smart," Howard said, and they began a long-distance romance.

From Quantico, Howard was transferred to Camp Lejeune in North Carolina, where he was stationed for the rest of his marine years. He had already graduated from Albany Law School, but he also had to spend two months on temporary additional duty studying military law in Newport, Rhode Island.

Driving back from Newport to Camp Lejeune, according to Howard, "It started snowing after an hour, and it started snowing hard." When he reached New York City, he decided to stay overnight. "The last thing I wanted to do was bang up my brand-new car." He rented a room in a cheap hotel near Times Square, and then headed back to the marines the next day.

Howard and Gerrie married in September. "I was in Camp Lejeune at the time," he said, "and I took two weeks off. I went home, got married, honeymooned in Bermuda, and went back to Camp Lejeune. Gerrie took care of her sick mother, and then came down to Camp Lejeune."

Together they raised seven children, all of whom enjoyed the benefit of Gerrie's love. They also had Howard as a role model—a man who has enjoyed success in just about everything he's ever done, including his tenure as an attorney in the military.

Assigned as a defense lawyer, Howard didn't take long to

make a major impression in the marines. "I got four straight acquittals in the Marine Corps, which is unheard of because with court-martials, there's no way they favor the defendant," he explained. "The fourth acquittal happened at about seven thirty one night."

The next morning, Howard reported back to his office at seven o'clock. The intercom rang ten minutes later. It was Colonel Maurice Goodpasture, head of the legal office staff of the Second Marine Division and a combat veteran of World War II and Korea. Goodpasture told Howard to come to his office. When Howard got there, he stood at attention and said, "Good morning, Colonel."

Goodpasture said, "Good morning, Howard. I heard you got another acquittal." Howard thought he saw a smirk on Goodpasture's face. The colonel continued, "Do you enjoy being a defense lawyer?" Before Howard could respond, Goodpasture said, "Don't answer the question. You are now working in the prosecutor's office."

"Yes, sir," said Howard. As he explained sixty years later, "I didn't have any choice."

But he did have one more case as a defense attorney. Three weeks after Goodpasture changed his job, Howard got an evening phone call from Captain Ralph McIlhenny of Company D, Second Division. "He was a Naval Academy graduate, a very capable guy," Howard said. McIlhenny was in deep trouble, as Howard explained. "There was a mock war in the Smokey Mountains in North Carolina. They were supposed to attack at the top of the mountain at five in the morning. McIlhenny was sent a memo telling him not to take any mobile transportation. But then McIlhenny sprained his ankle the night before. The weather was terrible, terrible. He tried unsuccessfully to get ahold of Colonel Charles Barrett. McIlhenny had to commandeer a jeep to get there, since he couldn't walk. He took a jeep up there, and he was court-martialed for disobeying an order."

McIlhenny asked Howard if he could see him the following morning. When they met, McIlhenny asked Howard to represent him. Howard told him that he had just been moved to the prosecutor's office, but that he would ask Colonel Goodpasture for permission. When Howard told him McIlhenny's story, Goodpasture told Howard to go ahead and defend him for that trial only.

At the court-martial, Howard cross-examined Colonel Barrett, who didn't like the questions. "He jumped out of the witness chair and started walking toward me," Howard said. "He was so angry. I said to the judge of the Court of Inquiry, Colonel Thomas, 'Colonel Barrett is out of order.' The judge looked at me, and then looked at Barrett and said, 'Colonel Barrett, you're out of order. Go back to the witness chair.'"

But Howard wasn't done with him. "I continued to cross-examine him. I was really getting into him. Then I brought in a dozen enlisted sergeants, all of whom had served in Korea and had been at a famous battle, the Frozen Chosin—a seventeen-day battle in freezing weather at the Chosin Reservoir in November 1950. Every one of them testified that weather conditions were worse at the exercise than in Korea." Colonel Thomas stopped the inquiry. No disciplinary action was taken. "Now I'm a hero," Howard said.

Indeed. Five weeks later, Howard received a letter of commendation, which went in his official record, from General James "Phil" Berkeley, Colonel Thomas's superior officer and the commanding general of the Second Marine Division. "I was the only lawyer in three and half years to get a letter of commendation," Howard said, still proud so many years later.

But the kudos kept coming. A month later, Howard was at

a party, talking to some friends, when someone asked him to talk to General James "Phil" Berkeley, who wanted to thank him personally for his work on McIlhenny's case. "He talked to me for about twenty minutes," Howard said. "Everyone saw me talking to the general."

Howard's barracks "cred" was off the charts. Then he was asked by Goodpasture, who was ill and in the hospital, to replace him in a case against a marine in Tokyo. "I was advising General Berkeley on court-martials," Nolan said. "I got to be good friends with the commanding general." Needless to say, Howard's time in the marines couldn't have gone much better.

"I had a great life experience in the Marine Corps," he said. "It was a great learning experience about people. You're living with forty-nine people going through basic training, four to a suite. We had two guys from New York, me and Bob Olson from the Bronx. He was a Little All-American in football at Catawba College, which is now North Carolina College. The other two guys were from Louisiana, and they couldn't have been more different from us. Robert Odom was from Angola, Louisiana, and James Murphree's father was an oil man in Shreveport. James went to Yale. We had four different backgrounds, but we wound up becoming very good friends.

"Odom was quite a character," said Howard, "right wing, but we both liked baseball. When we went to a Senators' game, he made a comment about Catholics storing guns in the basements of their churches to take over the United States. That was ridiculous. I said, 'Bob, come on, I thought we were friends.'" Then their conversation shifted to their futures, and Howard said that he was going back to Albany to practice law. "Odom said he'd have it made in one year. He also said that his cousin, Jimmy Davis, a country singer, would become governor of Louisiana." Davis did become the "singing governor" of Louisiana.

More than three decades after his conversation with Odom, Howard was meeting with Al Gore, who was running in the presidential Democratic primary against Bill Clinton in 1992. Gore had just come from New Orleans. Howard picked him up at the airport and they were driving to Michael's in Latham, just outside Albany, for dinner. Howard asked, "How's your campaign going there?"

Gore replied, "I have a great guy down there, the agriculture commissioner."

"What's his name?" Howard asked.

"Bob Odom."

Howard is still trying to wrap his mind around that one.

Chapter 6

NOLAN AND HELLER AND
REAL ESTATE, TOO

Leaving little to chance, Howard, who passed the bar in 1958, secured a job well before he finished his tenure with the marines in December 1960. That April, he took advantage of an offer from the law firm of Drislane and Walker. "Jim Drislane was a neighbor of mine and Mark's," Howard said. "I went to work with them." Howard spent three years with Drislane and Walker while doubling as the part-time assistant corporation counsel for the City of Albany.

Then Art McGinn, a lawyer in Albany who had graduated from Holy Cross three years before Howard, had an opening when his partner, Bob Luddy, another Holy Cross alum, died in an automobile accident. Six months later, McGinn offered Howard a full partnership in his practice. "I thought about it for a while," Howard said. "When I told Jim Drislane, he offered me a partnership, but I had already accepted the offer from Art." Howard lasted just nine months with McGinn, who became embroiled in a controversy with National Commercial Bank, which had hired McGinn and Nolan to do collection work.

In 1965, Howard decided to go out on his own. With

Drislane's help, he got an office in the same building. Howard immediately got the National Commercial Bank gig, and then quickly picked up business from a variety of entities ready to hire the hotshot marine lawyer. "We started doing collection work for real estate businesses, banks, and corporations," he said. "I was doing all their collection work. You'd get a percentage of the money you got back. The income kept getting bigger and bigger." That's called a good problem.

Using two full-time secretaries, Howard was as busy as he could be. "I was really stretched out. I used to go to lunch with Mark [Heller], and one day I said to him, 'Why don't you join me, and we'll become Nolan and Heller as partners?'"

Heller had attended Albany Academy, Hamilton College, and Harvard Law School. "He scored in the ninety-ninth percentile on the lawyers' aptitude test," Howard said. "Off the charts." After law school, Heller landed in New York City, becoming an attorney for the Port Authority. "Then he went with a law firm in New York City," Howard said. "He came back to Albany, working for Pennock and Roberts Law Firm."

Heller accepted Howard's offer, and three years later, he became an equal partner. "At first, I had a lot more business than him," Howard explained. Nolan and Heller opened in 1966, and then merged with Cooper, Erving and Savage, the oldest law firm in the state, in 1987. Cooper was the grandson of author James Fenimore Cooper, who wrote *The Leatherstocking Tales*. "Within a short period of time, we were one of the three biggest firms in the Capital District," Howard said.

Nolan and Heller would add on two equal partners—Tom Whalen, who would later become mayor of Albany, and Rich Weiner, who was summa cum laude at Union College and Phi Beta Kappa at Stanford Law School. "Not only was Rich very bright, but he had the personality to go with it," Howard said. "He did everything right. Very confident without being overconfident."

After three years with Nolan and Heller, Weiner asked Howard about becoming a partner. "I couldn't believe he said that," Howard said. "He was going to be jumping over other people. I talked to Mark in his office and told him about the conversation. Mark said, 'What do you think?' I said, 'Mark, I never thought I'd be saying this, but we should do it.' He said he felt the same way." Weiner became an equal partner.

Mark Heller's son Justin is now fifty-three and a comanaging partner in Nolan and Heller and also in Howard's real estate ventures. Justin said that Howard and his dad were "quite close. When I was growing up, my father, he didn't take work home with him a lot. There wasn't a lot of dinner talk about what he did."

Justin and Howard's son, Bob, have been friends since childhood. "I can remember us going with our two dads to an Army football game," Justin said. "When they formed their law firm, I'd go to their offices. I joined the firm when I got out of Albany Law School."

Regarding the relationship between his dad and Howard, Justin said, "They shared so much history. They were partners from 1966 to 1998 when my father retired. They were also business partners. They weren't the same type of person. My father was scholarly, while Howard is gregarious and outgoing. I think they complemented each other and respected each other's qualities. That's why they were such a good team. Howard brought them in, and my father did high-quality legal work."

Joyce Roman, who was Howard's administrative assistant in the senate and office manager at Nolan and Heller, said, "Mark Heller was a wonderful man. He and Howard were like brothers. They truly were."

Justin has grown closer to Howard since Mark's passing in April 2012. "Howard was very upset," Justin said. "I actually spend a lot of time with him. Howard and I are in much closer contact than we had been previously."

Asked how Howard keeps going at the age of eighty-five, Justin said, "It's remarkable, very remarkable. I think he's a tough, driven person. He will doggedly pursue his objective. He's always fair and pleasant to deal with, but at the same time, my sense was—and still is—that he knows what his goals are. He doesn't give up, and he has very good focus. He's determined to achieve the result he's after, whether in business, politics, or law, but with a smile on his face. He's personable with a friendly demeanor. It's very impressive when you can be friendly and tough at the same time."

Although Nolan and Heller was quickly successful, Howard decided that real estate might be more lucrative. "I started the law firm, and we did very well. But financially you can't make too much in the law business because you bill by the hour," Howard said. "So I was fortunate to get involved in real estate." He was also fortunate to have two great partners in real estate, Mark Heller and Norris "Mac" MacFarland, who operated MacFarland Builders and MacFarland Construction. "Mac was the second-largest construction contractor in the Capital District and my first major law client," Howard said.

Howard, Mark, and MacFarland formed HMC Associates and began acquiring properties. "We bought quite a bit of real estate all around the country—Memphis, Minneapolis," Howard said. "We were all over the place. The year before I ran for the senate in '73, we bought Delaware Plaza and Plattsburgh Plaza, which we still own; the Glengate Shopping Center in South Glens Falls; almost one hundred acres of land just south of Bethlehem Central High School in Delmar;

forty acres of wetland next to the Normanside Country Club and Office Plaza; and sixty acres of vacant land in Rensselaer. All these properties had been owned by wealthy people in New York City who were getting elderly and decided to sell everything. We never did meet them. We assumed mortgages on all the operating properties, and then we borrowed a substantial amount of money."

The investments were sound and generated revenue for Howard for the rest of his life. MacFarland's second wife, Peggy, worked part-time for Howard for two years, and she's now a limited partner in both shopping plazas. "That was part of my divorce settlement from Mac," she said. "He gave me limited partnerships in four different things to generate the income I needed to live."

She couldn't be a bigger fan of Howard. "I think he's a wonderful, wonderful person," she said. "I can't praise him enough. He was an honest senator. He was hardworking. He's a man of great faith, his Catholic faith. He would do anything for his friends. Anything. You only have to ask." Peggy is also impressed with Shannon and noted, "Whenever Howard refers to Shannon, he says, 'I've got the best wife in the world.' They are very good together."

In 1983, Delaware Plaza got a major uplift while adding seven new stores, including Flah's Country Curtain and Fashion Bug. Upgrades included installation of energy-efficient lighting and redoing the parking lot. "The plaza is now in its twenty-first year, so many of the original twenty-year leases are expiring, which gives us the chance to make some real changes and improvements," Norris MacFarland told Ann Treadway of the *Spotlight* in a November 23 story.

Howard shared this story about Woolworth's: "The real estate manager in New York and I had become friendly, and their lease was coming up. I talked to him about increasing his rent, which we had to do, and he said his boss, Victor Krulak, said no. Well, I met his boss a month later in his office outside Philadelphia. We start talking about the lease, and he's giving me a hard time. I finally pounded my fist on his desk and said, 'Sir, we had an old saying in the marines. The seven *P*s: proper prior planning prevents piss poor performance. Why isn't Woolworth's doing this? We have a great plaza and we want you to stay a long time.' He motioned me to come behind his desk and showed me a plaque on the wall saluting Major General Victor Krulak of the US Marines. The guy was highly decorated, and he wound up giving me everything I wanted on the lease."

Both Delaware Plaza and Plattsburgh Plaza continue to thrive to this day. "The two plazas are worth a lot more now than they were then," Howard said. "We sold the Normanside Plaza seven years ago for quite a handsome profit."

Howard wasn't as successful with the first two of three restaurants he bought.

When Howard ran for the New York State Senate for the first time in 1974, his district included most of Albany County, except the city of Cohoes, and Greene County. "The first time I ran, I didn't know anybody in Greene County," Howard said. So his buddy and political ally Dick Conners introduced him to Rayfield "Rafie" Klein, who was active in the Greene County Democratic Party. "Rafie ran my campaign in Greene County the first time I ran," Howard said. "Rafie and I became very close personal friends."

Through Rafie, Howard met Guy Chirico, who owned a motel and restaurant at Hunter Mountain, a popular skiing destination in the Catskills. "Guy wanted to open a restaurant in Catskill, about thirty miles south of Albany," Howard said. "He'd run it, but he needed partners to buy in." Howard, Chirico, and Rafie each took a quarter, and another Greene

County businessman, Orville Slutzky, bought the other quarter. "We bought a building, a big old colonial home, in downtown Catskill," Howard said. "We remodeled it and we called the restaurant the President's Wedding, because Martin Van Buren had gotten married and lived there. It was the most expensive restaurant around Catskill, and it started out pretty good. But eventually we started losing money, and we wound up selling it at a loss."

Howard laughed thinking about it, maybe because it didn't prevent him from buying a second restaurant. In 1991, he went 50-50 with Lee Aronowitz, his campaign manager and dear friend, and Lee's wife, Marcia, on a restaurant in downtown Albany called the Old State House. The building was owned by Joe Gerrity, a friend of Howard's who owned Saratoga Harness and both Standardbreds and Thoroughbreds. They renamed the restaurant The Entertainer.

Howard and Lee had met on a basketball court when Howard was in the eighth grade at Christian Brothers Academy. CBA was playing Milne for the city championship, and Aronowitz was one of Milne's top players. Lee and Howard also played golf and tennis against each other years later. They reconnected when Howard joined the Junior Chamber of Commerce, of which Lee was the president. "Lee and I became very good friends," Howard said. "He was a partner in Anchor Agency, a large insurance company, and he was very successful. He also became a partner in a tennis club in Latham."

Howard quickly learned several things about his new restaurant. "We made a mistake when we bought it. It was on a one-way street and we didn't have the proper amount of parking. And it turned out the heating didn't work great. And the air-conditioning system wasn't great." Those were strikes one, two, and three. "We started losing money, then more money," Howard said. "I told Lee that we ought to admit this is a losing proposition. He wanted to invest more money, but I said no. He finally agreed with me and we closed the restaurant. We had it for two years, but we had to stop the hemorrhaging."

Howard was undeterred by going zero-for-two with eating establishments. On January 8, 1990, he and John McDaniel, his twenty-five-year-old partner and a classmate of Howard's son, Bob, from Christian Brothers Academy and Le Moyne College, purchased an Albany landmark. The Orchard Restaurant & Tavern had first opened in 1905 on North Manning Avenue in Albany, and it was known by generations for its pizza, burgers, and sandwiches. "They had the best club sandwich I've ever eaten," Howard said. "Everything was good."

Howard told Caitlin Brown of the *Times Union*, "I've been going there since I was a kid. It just looked like an interesting thing to get involved with as an investor." McDaniel had been a bartender there as a college student.

Two days before Howard took over, more than four hundred people had crammed into the restaurant for a bash given by departing owner Michael Hickey, who had bought the restaurant thirteen and a half years earlier with his parents, John and Carmela Hickey. "I was friendly with Mike Hickey and his father," Howard said.

Howard kept the working manager, Mike Noonan, and eventually sold the Orchard Tavern to him in 1997. Financially, Howard did okay with that investment. If you add in all the free meals he had at the Orchard, Howard had finally found a restaurant investment he could stomach.

Chapter 7

JFK, RFK, AND A TASTE OF POLITICS

When Howard was a quarterback and safety on the freshman football team at Holy Cross, he had played against Ted Kennedy, an offensive and defensive end for Harvard. "I knew who he was at the time," Howard said. Two years later, Howard worked on the campaign of Ted's brother John F. Kennedy when he successfully ran against Henry Cabot Lodge for the US Senate in Massachusetts in 1952.

Howard got to know Ted and John's brother Robert F. Kennedy much better twelve years later. "I was attracted to the Kennedys because of their interest in public service," he said. "Being Catholic, I was very interested. But as time went by, I became disillusioned with Ted Kennedy. Robert Kennedy was a straight arrow. He was probably the smartest of the Kennedys."

When JFK won the 1960 presidential election, he appointed his brother Bobby to be US attorney general. "The first person Robert hired was John Nolan—no relation—a partner in a Washington, DC, law firm, to be his executive assistant and basically run the daily business in the attorney general's office," Howard said. After JFK was assassinated in

November 1963, Bobby decided to run for the US Senate in New York against the incumbent Ken Keating.

One of John Nolan's closest friends was Art McGinn. They had served in the marines together in Korea and been classmates at Georgetown Law School. Art McGinn happened to be Howard's law partner in Albany. A week before the 1964 Democratic Convention at the Sixty-Ninth Street Armory in Manhattan, John Nolan invited McGinn to the convention. When McGinn asked if he could bring a couple of friends, John Nolan said yes. McGinn invited Howard, who had been to one convention in Syracuse, and another friend, Carroll Mealy, to join him. At the time, Howard was a practicing lawyer for McGinn and Nolan and the assistant corporation counsel for the City of Albany.

Howard went to the convention. After Bobby got the nomination, Howard was invited to a cocktail party at the Stattler Hilton on Seventh Avenue. "That's how I first met Bobby Kennedy," he said. "We also met some of his kids." Howard returned to Albany that night. Two days later, John Nolan called McGinn to tell him he was leaving his position in the attorney general's office to run Bobby's campaign. "The first guy Bobby hired was John Nolan," Howard said. "He ran Bobby's campaign. Everything went through John Nolan."

And John had an offer for Howard—spend two months working on Bobby's campaign. Howard was intrigued, but it would mean leaving his current positions. The private one was no big deal, but leaving the city Corporation Counsel was a whole different scenario. "Corning wasn't enthusiastic about me doing it because he didn't like Robert Kennedy," Howard said. But Corning didn't have final say— Dan O'Connell did. O'Connell told Howard that it was okay to take the two months off and work for Kennedy. "Outside of O'Connell, Corning was God, but Corning bowed to O'Connell," Howard said.

Howard was thirty-three. "I was an enrolled Democrat, but not an active Democrat. Kennedy was a long shot when he entered the race." But Howard wasn't opposed to supporting long shots, human or equine. He saw Kennedy blossom as a public speaker and a politician. "I spent a lot of time in New York working for him. Right in the beginning, Robert Kennedy made a speech in Harlem, and he stuttered and hesitated. By the time the campaign was over, however, he was a great public speaker. It was interesting. The battleground in New York City for the senatorial race was Queens. At the time, Queens went back and forth, Democrat and Republican. I spent the last two weeks of the campaign working with Matt Ryan, a good friend of Robert Kennedy's."

While campaigning on the West Side of Manhattan, Howard got a thrill of a lifetime. "My job was to run the last rally of the day at the Theresa Hotel on Third Avenue," he said. "I organized the rally—and who comes along in a big limousine but Governor Averill Harriman." Never bashful, Howard went over to introduce himself and shake hands with the governor. The first thing Harriman told Howard was "Son, don't ever shake a politician's hand so strong." Howard's dad had told him to shake hands firmly.

Harriman gave his speech to support Kennedy, and then Kennedy said to Howard, "Come on, Governor Harriman wants to go to his hotel, the Carlyle." So Howard climbed into Harriman's limo. "On one side of me was Robert Kennedy and on the other was Governor Harriman. I just listened. There I was, a young lawyer sitting in the backseat of a limo with the attorney general and the governor. It was quite a thrill, to say the least. It was very early in the race."

Harriman had an apartment at the Carlyle. He got out

and shook hands with Howard, much more gently this time. "Kennedy turned to me and said, 'Governor Harriman has done more for my campaign than anybody. He raised a lot of money.'" Then Howard accompanied Kennedy to his headquarters on Forty-Second Street between Fifth and Sixth Avenues. "Kennedy went to get something to eat with his wife and his three older boys," Howard said. "One of his sons sat in his lap. The only people he talked to during the lunch were his three kids. That impressed me a lot. There were a lot of important people in the room. The kids had to be ten, eleven, and twelve. They obviously had a close relationship with their father. Of course, that got snuffed out four years later when Kennedy was shot."

Howard spent the final two weeks of the campaign in Queens. "It was a great thrill for me, meeting some of the people I met. It was a very unusual thing for somebody my age. Kennedy was a long shot when he entered the race, but Lyndon Johnson won in New York big-time—and in the end, Kennedy won convincingly."

Buoyed by that experience, Howard could have jumped into Albany politics, but he did not. "It's interesting how life is," he said. "There was a lot of corruption in Albany. I was not so happy about representing the City of Albany. I was so busy privately, and I'd shake my head about things the city did." So Howard resigned from the Corporation Counsel in 1965, three years after he had started as a part-timer.

It's hard to know how Corning interpreted Howard's action, which obviously signified that he had no interest in getting involved in Albany politics. Their long, love-hate relationship took an unexpected turn a week after Howard resigned, when Corning called and asked him to come to his office.

Twenty-two years earlier, Howard, then eleven, Mark

Heller, and other neighborhood friends had walked into Corning's office. They had asked him to build a baseball diamond, and he had.

Howard had potentially angered the mayor when he went over his head to get O'Connell's okay to spend two months working on Kennedy's campaign, and then had quit his job as the city's assistant corporate counsel. Was that why Corning called him to his office?

No, Corning was looking forward, not backward, and he needed Howard's help. So Corning hired Howard as a private attorney. A new state law, the Municipal Annexation Law, allowed the City of Albany to expand in size—and, of course, create new voters—by seizing land. "Corning was the godfather of the law," Howard said. "He was a brilliant guy."

Corning was proposing to annex land from the Town of Bethlehem. This attempted annexation would be the first in the state. "When I took a look at what the mayor wanted done, I suggested two annexations," Howard said. "One would be the southern end of Whitehall Road to the Thruway, then a second to include a much larger area. My reasoning was that the first was a slam dunk. It wasn't a very big annexation. There was no way we could lose that. The second one included Normanskill Creek and was very large."

Howard took another step forward, requesting both cases be tried at the same time. The appellate division appointed three New York State Supreme Court judges, including Presiding Judge Mike Sweeney, to hear the case. "All Republicans," Howard said. "In those days, all the supreme court judges in upstate were Republican. Sweeney asked the most questions and the other two went along with him, no matter what he said."

Three months later, the court ruled on both cases, giving the land to the City of Albany. Corning had won. "He told so many people that I was the best lawyer in Albany," Howard said.

Howard wasn't finished winning annexation cases. "I got calls from all over the state," he said. "The first guy to call me was Jerry Markowitz, the mayor of Middletown in Orange County. He called me out of the blue. He and I became very friendly. His oldest son came to work for Nolan and Heller. He did tax law."

Howard won three cases for Markowitz on the way to winning twenty-one straight annexation cases, representing Saratoga Springs, Amsterdam, the villages of Highland Falls and Irvington, and the towns of Norwich and Oneonta.

Corning wasn't through using Howard's attorney expertise. "We [the Corporation Council's Office] were the lawyers for the City of Albany's Board of Education," Howard said. The board of education had just been sued by Lola Johnson Cole, an African American teacher at Philip Schuyler High School from September 1964 through June 1966, who had been denied tenure by Principal Ben Becker. Cole's suit alleged she had been denied tenure because of her race.

Becker was one of the most beloved coaches, teachers, and administrators in the entire Capital District, a man who had coached legendary boxer Muhammad Ali (then known as Cassius Clay) to Olympic Gold in the 1960 Olympics in Rome, started a camp for needy youngsters, and helped hundreds of other kids. In recommending that Cole not receive tenure, Becker had written in a May 17, 1966, letter that she was uncooperative, frequently tardy for her homeroom assignments, and failed to attend two supervisors' meetings.

"There was no way he was prejudiced," Howard said. "The mayor wanted me to handle it." So Howard solicited a letter from Ali on Becker's behalf. He brought in a slew of prominent black citizens, including Nebraska Brace, a popular member of the city council from Arbor Hill who had boxed and been coached by Becker. Brace would wind up working for Howard for twenty years. "I brought in several others," Howard said. "It was a steady parade, including a lot of minorities testifying how unprejudiced Becker was. We wound up winning the case, and twice she appealed the decision. The verdict stood. Of course, after that, Ben said that I was a god, what a great lawyer I was."

Corning couldn't have been happier with Howard when the case was finally over. But he wasn't quite as happy years later when Howard decided to run for the senate representing Albany and Greene Counties. Corning then went after Howard big-time, when Howard had the guts to vote for a different candidate than Corning's choice for senate minority leader. Then Howard cemented Corning's disapproval by taking him on in the 1977 mayoral primary, the one and only time anyone in the Democratic Party would challenge the longest-tenured mayor in American history.

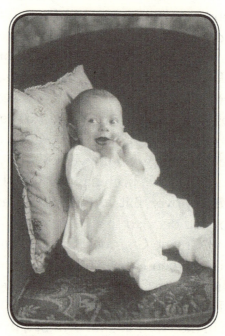

Howard as an infant in 1932

Howard on pony Mickey, and his dad

Howard and his parents

Howard with his baby sister, Mary Beth

Mary and Kevin Langan (front), and Dorothy and Victor Oberting

Howard, Lee, and Marcia Aronowitz, Rita and Bob Slocum

Mark and Carolyn Heller

Howard, Jim Mulcahy, and Norris MacFarland

Ruth Logan, Shannon's mom; sister Marcia; Shannon; and sisters Mary and Shasta (Credit Tom Brander)

The Nolan children (left to right): Anne, Debbie, Bob, Kathy, Karen, Lynn, and Donna

Howard's daughters (left to right): Lynn, Donna, Anne, Karen,
Kathy. Howard and Debbie (front)

Howard and his son, Bob

Grandson Nolan Cummings and Howard

Chapter 8

THE FIRST TIME

One of Howard's dad's closest friends—and a friend of Howard's, too—was Dick Conners, one of the most popular politicians in Albany's history. Known as the "dean of the assembly," Conners was a lifelong resident of Albany. He spent fifty years in political office before he died in June 1995 at the age of eighty-five.

Conners's life and career centered on Albany's North End and the Irish-American neighborhood surrounding Sacred Heart Church. A graduate of Christian Brothers Academy, Conners attended Albany Business College and headed the insurance brokerage firm founded by his father in 1895.

Conners began his political career as an alderman on the Albany City Council in 1942, the same year Erastus Corning served his first of forty-two-plus years as mayor. Conners represented the same ward that his father, Michael Conners, had represented in the 1880s. After twenty years as an alderman, Conners was elected city council president, a position he held for sixteen years. Then he won the first of eight consecutive, two-year terms in the New York State Assembly representing the 104th District. Conners concentrated on issues critical to veterans and the elderly. He sponsored legislation extending the statute of limitations for Vietnam veterans with health problems linked to Agent Orange.

Despite the fact that Howard had been trending away from the Albany Democratic machine because of its blatant corruption and favoritism, he worked on Dick Conners's campaign for the US Congress in 1972, a mission Conners really didn't want. "Dick had no interest in Congress; he wanted to stay local," Howard said. "What happened was that a week before the nomination meeting, Leo O'Brien didn't want to run for Congress anymore. He was in his last year. When Erastus Corning found that out, they had to come up with a candidate. Everybody was advising him on different people. He wanted Dick Conners. Dick wasn't happy, but he was a true party person. That's how he wound up running for Congress. Everybody loved Dick Conners. He was one of my dad's closest friends. We had lunch once a week."

Conners would barely lose his election to Dan Button. In the interim, Conners went to bat for Howard.

"I'm sitting in my office on an early Friday afternoon in March and I get a phone call from Dick Conners," Howard said. "He says he just got a call from Charlie Mufale, a ward leader in the South End of Albany better known as 'Charlie the Barber' who had met with Dan O'Connell, and they wanted me to run for the New York State Senate. Completely out of the blue. In 1974, Walter Langley was the three-term incumbent state senator representing Albany and Greene Counties. He was a lawyer, a Republican, and a friend of mine. Good guy."

More pertinent was that Howard had been distancing himself from the Democratic machine, though he had been active in the Albany community through the Cerebral Palsy Foundation, the Junior Chamber of Commerce, and Pop Warner Football. "I told him, 'Dick, you know how I feel about the organization,'" Howard said. "We talked and talked. He said, 'Why don't you go home and think about it? I think you'd be a great senator.'"

So Howard considered the offer over the weekend. Back in 1966 he had sent Democratic leaders a feeler for a seat in either the senate or the assembly. "I had thought it was time for a change. Unfortunately, the leaders didn't," he said. Now, eight years later, the party leaders had come to him. "The more I thought about it, with my love for politics, it would be a heck of an opportunity."

Howard did have intelligence on his prospective opponent, attorney Walter Langley, a fifty-three-year-old, three-time incumbent in the senate from 1969 to 1974. Langley's law partner, John Kinum, was a friend of Howard's from law school. "He had mentioned to me in a casual conversation that Walter had been sick a lot," Howard said. "It was in the paper. He'd been in the hospital for a month. I thought that if I ran, Walter might not be healthy enough to run or decide not to run."

He then had a discussion with Mark Heller, his lifelong friend and legal and real estate partner. If Howard ran for office, it meant a lot of time away from the firm Nolan and Heller—and even more time away if he won. "Obviously, I wasn't going to do it without him agreeing that I should do it," Howard said. "Mark was all for it. He loved politics."

Howard called Conners on Monday morning and told him he was interested. Conners called back and told Howard that O'Connell was very happy with Howard's decision and wanted to see him right away. They set up a visit for that evening. "Dick asked me if I wanted him to go with me, which I did," Howard said. "The two of us went over to Dan's house at seven o'clock that evening. Dan was eighty-nine. I picked Dick up in North Albany and rang the doorbell. I said, 'Dick, you go in first. I haven't seen him in six years.' Charlie Mufale answered the door. Charlie cooked O'Connell's dinner several nights a week. O'Connell was in his chair watching the TV in his living room."

Howard walked in and said, "Mr. Chairman, it's been a long time. I appreciate your offer to run for the senate."

Dan said, "I think you can be a good senator. We wanted Tom Brown to run, but he didn't want to because he was running for reelection as an assemblyman."

O'Connell told Howard to talk to some of the machine's players with his blessing, and the biggest player happened to be the mayor of Albany. "One of the first people I saw was Erastus," Howard said. "He wasn't encouraging.

I had broken with him two or three years earlier because of my friendship with Larry Kahn, who had changed parties."

Corning preferred a different candidate, Leonard Weiss, who had lost the election in 1972. Weiss, a friend of Howard's who ultimately became a New York State Supreme Court justice, was friends with Corning's confidante, Polly Noonan. "When they found out I was going to be the candidate, they thought Leonard should be the candidate instead," Howard said.

Howard got a call from Jimmy Ryan, the secretary of the Albany County Democratic Committee. "He tells me, 'Dan wants you to announce right away' because he was getting pressure," Howard said. "I knew where it was coming from."

Howard acted quickly, calling the media. "There was a hastily called press conference the next morning right in front of Key Bank at 60 State Street. I made a short speech that I was running for the senate. During the press conference, they asked if I had Dan's blessing. That was the first question I was asked. I said I did."

The press conference didn't last long. "Most of the media ran over to Whitehall Road to see Dan O'Connell," Howard said. "Most of the press didn't know me. Dan confirmed that I was the Democratic candidate." He could almost hear Corning's blood pressure rising.

The first phone call Howard made after the announcement of his candidacy on the six o'clock news was to his dear friends Lee and Marcia Aronowitz. "They were very close friends of mine," Howard said. "Lee was a real people person and a very competitive guy, as I am."

Marcia said of her late husband of thirty-seven years, "They [Lee and Howard] were really best friends. They were so civic minded. My husband, I never heard him swear. He could make anyone laugh, and he was as smart as hell. He really understood politics."

Howard asked both Lee and Marcia to help him on the campaign, and they jumped aboard, as did Heller. "Then I started forming a campaign team," Howard said.

Lee became Howard's campaign manager. He was close enough to Howard that when Howard began wandering off point at a press conference or during an interview, Lee would give him the choke sign to cut it off. "It happened all the time," Marcia said, laughing.

On June 12, Howard and other Democrats were officially nominated for office at the Polish Community Center. Arlene Bigos covered the event for the *Knickerbocker News*:

> The mood was happy, helped by the liquor that was flowing from the bar at the rear of the hall as about 800 Albany County Democrats chose their candidates Wednesday night for the November election. Albany Mayor Corning congratulated Howard C. Nolan, the party's choice for state senator, on giving the meeting

a "nice touch" after he staged the only demon-
stration of the evening. As Nolan was nominated, several children, including a few of
Nolan's seven offspring, paraded around the
Polish Community Center, led by a boy (his
son Bob) with a microphone chanting, "We
want Nolan."

The children distributed posters to the crowd
displaying their slogans "Zowie Howie," "We
want Nolan' and "Nolan for Senator'" While
the crowd listened and voted on other nominations, Nolan workers pasted Nolan bumper
stickers on every car in the parking lot. Nolan,
who came on stage and waved to the crowd
as his marchers shouted his name, had a ram-
bunctious acceptance speech in his pocket
but was not given the opportunity to use it.
Many Democrats stayed to drink to victory in
November.

Bigos had broken a story two weeks earlier that said
Howard had been contacted by Republicans in 1969 to run for
mayor against Corning. "I was sitting on a beach in San Juan,
Puerto Rico, when I got a phone call to oppose Corning,"
Howard had told Bigos. "The call came out of the blue and I
was shocked. I decided to remain a Democrat and not run."

Five years later, the Republican he was running against
for New York State Senate changed. On June 3, Langley, who
would die two years later, announced he would not seek reelection because of his health. Instead, the Republican Party
placed a mountain in front of Howard—the highly successful businessman Carl Touhey, the owner of Orange Motor
Corporation, who had run against Corning for mayor in 1973

and lost by just 3,552 votes, Corning's smallest winning margin in his forty-two-year career.

Howard couldn't have been a bigger long shot, and he quickly found out just how difficult his battle was going to be. He called Dick Barrett, a worker for the City of Albany Parks Department. "Dick ultimately was probably as valuable as anybody on my team," Howard said. "He was a young guy, but a political buff, very good with numbers. One of the things he'd done on and off was study polling. He wound up doing all my polling. A very bright guy. He was a deadly accurate pollster and very, very helpful in that sphere. I'll never forget the first poll we did."

It was a name recognition poll of Nolan and Touhey. "I was under the impression that I had high recognition in the city of Albany," Howard said. "A top athlete, president of the Junior Chamber of Commerce, CEO and chairman of the board for the Cerebral Palsy Center." But Howard was living in fiction. "We did the poll, and 7 percent of the people knew my name. That was a shocker."

Touhey's number was not. He had nearly pulled off the biggest upset in Albany political history. "He was the toughest opponent I ever ran against," Howard said. And the best known—his name recognition was 90 percent. "I looked at his figure and my figure and said, 'Oh, my God.' He obviously had a big edge going in."

Another man might have crumbled, but Howard Nolan was not that man. "I immediately thought that it was an aberration," he said. "So the first conclusion I came to was that I had to get back to a more normal Democratic vote in the city of Albany. That was going to be key—that and only taking a small loss in Colonie, which was historically Republican. Those were two places I had to step up. I knew a lot of people in Colonie because I'd been active in the Saint Ambrose and

Saint Pius parishes. That's where I had to concentrate, and that's what I did. Gerrymandering was regularly done, and the district had been redrawn to help Langley by eliminating the city of Cohoes, which was overwhelmingly Democratic, and changing Schoharie County, which was 50-50, to Greene County, which was heavily Republican."

Howard began campaigning the day after he got nominated, and he had lots of help. He didn't have to look far for volunteers, because he had seven children. "When he was running, we went door-to-door with him," said Debbie Nolan Murray, who now runs her family's two shopping plazas in Delmar and Plattsburgh. "He had a van, with a speaker, that had *Nolan* written all over it. He'd pack all seven of us in the van, and we'd go door-to-door. I was, like, seven the first time."

Debbie and her siblings enjoyed the experience. "He always made it fun," she said. "It wasn't a burden. We'd really enjoy it. He was always so positive and enthusiastic. It was good to see that aspect of him. We saw it at home. We thought it was pretty cool. I think we all felt that way."

Her sister Lynn sure did. "We had a blast," she said. After Howard won his first term, the Nolan kids had matching sweatshirts proclaiming, "Reelect my dad." Lynn had another sweatshirt made, but Howard told her not to wear it in public. It read, "I'm a Democrat. You're a Republican. Let's be friends. I'll hug your elephant if you kiss my ass." The sweatshirt had a picture of an elephant and a donkey. "It was the best sweatshirt ever," Lynn said.

Howard began campaigning daily door-to-door, armed with insights gained from working on Robert Kennedy's senatorial campaign. "Essentially, I campaigned seven days a week," Howard said. "I walked past probably every house and building in the city of Albany, ringing doorbells, and in the town of Colonie. I had a small group of several people with me every day, not the same people. I had advance people, a strategy that I had learned from the Kennedy campaign. One person went ahead, ringing the doorbell and telling them that Howard was coming. If nobody was home, move on to the second house.

"I'll never forget this. I'm campaigning in Colonie, off Red River Road. At one house, this guy comes out and says to me, 'Listen, I'm a Republican. I've never voted for a Democrat.' We had a brief discussion and I moved on. So we go down the street, around the corner, then come back on the other side of the street. When I get opposite this guy's house, he walks across the street and says, 'You know, I told you I'd never vote for a Democrat, but I never had a guy come to my door. After I thought about it, I'm going to give you a vote.'"

Not every volunteer on Howard's campaign was a family member or close friend. Philip Calderone was a sophomore majoring in political science at Siena College in Loudonville, two miles north of Albany. Calderone would go on to become Albany deputy mayor for Mayor Jerry Jennings for seventeen years, before being named deputy Albany County executive to Daniel McCoy on January 1, 2014. One of Calderone's college professors had told him that if he really wanted to learn about politics, he should volunteer for a local campaign. Just a few days later, Calderone's doorbell rang and there stood Howard Nolan, who was canvassing the uptown Albany neighborhood.

"This was the first or second day of my campaign," Howard said. "Phil answered the door, and I asked to see his parents. They came to the door, and I talked to them and then left. As I was walking up the street, I felt a tap on my shoulder. It was Phil Calderone. He asked if he could volunteer for me. I said, 'Sure.' He called me a day later."

Calderone not only volunteered for Howard, but also became a student intern in Howard's senate office and, while a student at Albany Law School, a clerk at Nolan and Heller. "Terrific guy, smart, very capable and very honest," Howard said. "I can't say enough good things about him. He did nothing but outstanding work."

Two Albany State seniors, John Hicks and Ed Reinfurt, who had been buddies growing up in Watervliet, received college credit for working on Howard's campaign after being recommended by Leonard Weiss. "I learned how to drive the van with a stick shift and bartend at his functions," said Reinfurt with a laugh. He was a 160-pound outside linebacker on the Albany State Great Danes football team. "We put together an eight-page newsletter to elect Howard Nolan. Lee Aronowitz was his campaign manager. Howard was such a positive, upbeat guy. We were learning as we went. There was no job too small, nothing too large. Howard was a happy warrior. It was just a fun group. He was a great campaigner. Obviously, he enjoyed it. He seemed so natural, a little Kennedy-esque, well dressed and polished."

Reinfurt, who was vice president of the Business Council of New York State and is a director of Pioneer Savings Bank in Colonie, became the youngest person elected to office in New York State history when he won a five-year term for the board of election in Watervliet. "The board refused to seat me," he said. "I was nineteen. Lenny Weiss was my attorney. I won, and then I became the youngest to retire five years later. I got to know Howard through Lenny."

John Hicks has had an interesting ride with Howard, whom he got to know through Ed Reinfurt. "That's how I met Howard," said Hicks, a successful attorney. "I went door-to-door. I drove his van around and had quite a time."

After Howard got elected in November 1974, Hicks, still

a student at Albany State, spent a week of winter break on a no-frills stay in Puerto Rico with one of his buddies. "We were staying in this shabby hotel," he said. "One morning, I was on the beach, near the hotel. Somebody poked me in the ribs. It was Howard."

"What are you doing here?" Howard asked.

"Just here for a week."

"Where are you staying?"

Hicks pointed back to the hotel and replied, "At that rat hole back there."

Howard then offered Hicks an opportunity. Howard had a condominium that he wasn't using. If Hicks would help Howard's maid clean the condominium the next day, Hicks could stay there the rest of the week. Hicks leaped at the offer.

Howard picked him up at six the next morning. Hicks, of course, had been out drinking the night before with his buddy. Howard told him, "Clean the place and I'll pick you up at three o'clock."

As Hicks related the story, "I was hung over. We cleaned the condo. The maid left. Three o'clock, no Howard. Four o'clock, no Howard. Five o'clock, no Howard. I had to take two buses to get back. Howard called the next morning and said, 'Something came up. I hope you're not pissed.'"

"Don't ever fucking call me again," Hicks answered, slamming the phone down.

But their relationship didn't end then. A decade or so later, Hicks, who had first attended the races at Saratoga when he was nine years old with his grandmother, had decided he wanted to get involved with owning Thoroughbreds. So he called Howard and they reconnected. Howard owned two yearlings that he was willing to split 50-50 with Hicks.

"I named one of them for Elizabeth, my daughter," Hicks said. His daughter's nickname was Tish, and Hicks had named that horse Tishmeister. On August 2, 2007, Tishmeister won the $150K Statue of Liberty for New York–breds at Saratoga. "It was one of the greatest thrills of my life," he said.

Hicks and Howard have partnered on many Thoroughbreds, including Irish Whisper, a daughter of Tishmeister, who earned $216,712. Their once-ruptured relationship remains tight even though Hicks, like many of Howard's friends, is a conservative Republican. "Howard's fantastic," Hicks said. "We share a box at Saratoga. He's got great drive and he works hard. He really connects with people, whether it's the janitor or the president. He came from humble beginnings, and I think he remembers his roots."

Eighteen years after Howard bought a share in Arcangues, and won the $3 million Breeders' Cup Classic in 1993, Hicks bought a 75 percent interest in Drosselmeyer a month before he captured the $5 million Breeders' Cup Classic in 2011.

Hicks sounded wistful while reflecting on the door-to-door campaigning he did on Howard's behalf: "I had a lot of fun and learned a lot about politics. And Howard got elected."

While ringing doorbell after doorbell, Howard, again dipping into the lessons he had learned in the Kennedy campaign, asked his volunteers to put Nolan bumper stickers on their cars. Then he added a twist, acting on an idea he got from Marcia Aronowitz. As she explained, "We went to the Cape that summer, and on the way we saw a lot of lawn signs in Massachusetts. We thought it was a great idea for Howard. We hadn't seen them in the Capital District. That's how we got Howard's name out."

Many days, Howard and his crew would work through the early evening. "A lot of the days, I wouldn't finish until nine o'clock at night. When I finished, I usually had four or five people with me." Frequently they dined at Sam's, a popular Italian restaurant on Southern Boulevard in Albany. Sam's would stay open until midnight back then. "I became a regular," Howard said. "My favorite dish was calamari. He made the best calamari. And anything with red sauce, because they still make the best red sauce." Howard and Shannon still dine at Sam's.

On August 24, the *Times Union* ran a large picture of Howard dribbling a ball with his back to Ticky Burden on an outdoor basketball court. Burden is an Albany high school legend who, at the time, was an All-American at the University of Utah. He would play in both the American Basketball Association and in the National Basketball Association. In the accompanying story, Joe Picchi wrote, "Howard Nolan can't make the jump shot like back in the old days when he was a basketball standout and starred in several sports for CBA. Nolan doesn't have to anymore." Ticky told Picchi he was endorsing Howard "because he is a longtime friend, a good sports enthusiast, and can do a wonderful job for the state of New York."

Howard's campaign began gaining momentum, and it wasn't slowed by a series of debates with Carl Touhey sponsored by various civic groups. "I must have debated Touhey eight or nine times," Howard said. "In mid-August, the *Times Union* interviewed Carl Touhey, maybe on the front page, and they had a picture of Touhey on his big boat in Newport, Rhode Island. He hadn't campaigned. When they asked why, he said he had just run for mayor and that he was going to start [campaigning] on Labor Day. He had spent most of the summer with his boat. And at every debate, at some point, I pulled out the clipping and intimated that obviously Touhey thinks he's a shoo-in. I showed the picture of him on the boat, and Carl got very angry about that."

Of course, support from the Democratic machine was

crucial, and it kept coming despite Corning's objections. "We spent a lot of money, and a lot of it came from the Albany County Democratic Party," Howard said. "At one point, at a dinner a month before the election at the Thruway House on Washington Avenue, I got there right at the end of the cocktail party. As I was walking in, Jimmy Ryan was talking to a couple of people. He wanted me to come over. He excused himself from the people he was talking to, and he looked at me and said, 'Erastus doesn't want to spend any more money on your campaign.' Then he added, 'No way that's going to happen. Dan wants to spend the money.'" They both laughed. Not even Corning dared to cross O'Connell.

As the election neared, Howard grew cautiously optimistic. "We continued to poll on a regular basis, and each poll showed me gaining strength. The last poll we did two weeks before Election Day showed me in the lead."

Shortly before the election, Howard and Touhey appeared at a fund-raiser at Kenwood Academy, a Catholic school in South Albany. "We were talking to Carl," Marcia Aronowitz said. "We all knew each other. One of Howard's daughters saw Touhey's pin on Carl's lapel and said, 'Touhey, yuck!' It was great. We all laughed. Carl laughed. He was a fine gentleman."

Howard spent Election Day saying hello to people around Albany. He had arranged a dinner for his closest supporters and family at the Desmond Americana Hotel in Colonie, where he waited for the results in a private room. "I started getting phone calls from polling places around nine thirty that night," he said. "It looked good right from the beginning. The media called the winner at ten thirty." Asked how hearing that felt, he said, "A lot of euphoria."

Howard won by more than six thousand votes—63,589 to 57,148, a bigger margin than Corning had had when he beat Touhey for mayor the previous year. Howard had received a major boost from Hugh Carey, his fellow Democrat, who won the race for governor over Malcolm Wilson. "Hugh Carey beat Malcolm Wilson quite handily," Howard said. "It was a big help to me because Carey ran strongly in Albany County."

He made his victory speech in the ballroom at the Americana. "It was quite an amazing night," Marcia said. "Everybody was thrilled. This was a big win. We weren't Erastus Corning Democrats—we were fix-the-city Democrats."

Howard thanked everyone. "Right after I finished my speech, who walked in? Carl Touhey, by himself, came over. He put his arm around me and said, 'Congratulations.' I was so impressed with the way he handled himself. He was a real impressive person. There was no question about it. I was truly impressed with that show of himself, the type of person he was."

Later that night, Touhey revealed to Gene Weingarten, a reporter for the *Knickerbocker News*, just how devastated he was by the loss to Howard. "I'm numb, just numb. I can't even think. I've lost twice. You run because you want to change things, and now I've lost twice."

But Howard, just like Touhey, had promised change if he was elected to represent the District of Albany in the New York State Senate. "My first priority is to reform the legislature, to open it up to the people," Howard told Weingarten in that same *Knickerbocker News* story. "If Republicans won't reform themselves, then I'll lay it right in their laps with a media campaign."

Howard's love/hate relationship with Corning, which had turned icy during Howard's victorious campaign, didn't take long to deteriorate to downright nasty. "I won the election, and then I got a phone call the next day from Fred Ohrenstein, who represented the lower west side of Manhattan, where we had a law office," Howard said. "Ohrenstein was a brilliant lawyer, a Harlan Fiske Stone Scholar at Columbia Law School, an ultra-liberal Democrat. His district included Greenwich Village. He called me and said he was going to throw his name in for senate minority leader. He wanted to talk to me."

Never opposed to hearing just about anyone's opinion on any topic, Howard met with Ohrenstein in Manhattan. "He told me what he wanted to do. I was impressed with a lot of his ideas," Howard said. "He'd come to be called L'Enfant Terrible [terrible child] for his long speeches advocating a liberal agenda that nobody wanted to hear about."

The pressure came quickly. Pat Cunningham, the state Democratic chairman and a friend of Hugh Carey, called to say that the new governor supported Jeremy Bloom from Brooklyn. "Cunningham asked me to support Bloom," Howard said. "Then I got a call from Erastus Corning saying, 'I'd like you to consider Jeremy Bloom.' Bloom's secretary was Polly Noonan, who had worked for Corning in the state senate six years earlier. I told Corning that I was going to support Ohrenstein, and he said, 'You're making a terrible mistake. You're the only person, or one of a few people, who's going to vote for Ohrenstein.'"

Howard had replied, "So be it." More than forty years later, Howard said, "I didn't really care what they thought."

State senate Democrats scheduled a meeting after Christmas to vote for minority leader. "As we got closer to the meeting, I was getting calls from Corning suggesting I vote for Bloom," Howard said. "Toward the end, I told him I was going to support Ohrenstein. This was two days before we were going to vote. He wasn't happy.

"Then I went down to New York," Howard continued. "The vote was going to be at ten o'clock in a conference room at the old Biltmore Hotel. Just before it started, I called my office and found out that I'd gotten a call from Doug Rutnik, a friend of mine who was married to Polly's daughter Penny, who had become very close to Corning. I called Doug back, and he said, 'I just came from the mayor's office and I've never seen him as mad as he is at you. He would like you to change your vote.' I said I was supporting Ohrenstein."

The vote on the second ballot was 15–10 for Ohrenstein, one vote more than he needed to win. "Corning didn't speak to me for two years," Howard said. "I'd say hello to him, and he'd turn his head. He was furious for the first two years I was in office. Fast-forward to 1976, two weeks before the nominations. Corning used to have his press conferences every Monday morning. One of the reporters said to him, 'We understand you haven't been friendly to Nolan. Are you going to support him two weeks from now?' Corning said, 'He's not going to get renominated.' Reporters went to see Dan O'Connell, who told them I would be the nominee. O'Connell told the reporters, 'It's just a family feud. It'll blow over.'"

At the Polish Community Center on Washington Avenue Extension, Howard won the 1976 nomination for the Forty-Second Congressional District in the state senate to run against thirty-eight-year-old Arnold Proskin, an attorney who had served two terms as Albany County district attorney and one year as Albany County court judge, a position he relinquished to take on Howard.

In his first term, Howard had served on several committees, including Finance, Cities, Local Governments, Mental Hygiene, and Commerce. He was also one of five senators picked in August 1975 to compile a proposed code of ethics for senators and assemblymen, which Ohrenstein would offer as a bill in 1976. "It got nowhere," Howard said.

In a thorough interview with both candidates in an article published in October 1976, the (Troy) *Times Record* asked them several intriguing questions, acknowledging that some people had called their campaign "bitter."

Asked how a senator balances the needs of the people in his district with the greater needs of the people in the state, Howard said, "You have to try to balance the two. If ever a conflict arises over a certain issue, you have to measure the two to see which is more important."

Howard spoke of working with Assemblyman Tom Brown (D-Albany) to get a $4 million appropriation for renovating the Port of Albany; leading the fight against *lulus*, a stipend for leadership duties that he donated to charity in his first year in the senate; and refusing to accept the stipend in his second year. Howard said one of his priorities was taxes: "We are the highest-taxed state in the nation, and we have to reverse that." He said he supported the recommendations of the Fleischman Commission for a complete state takeover of the cost of education, which would be funded by replacing the real property tax system with a statewide property tax. The true market value of property would be used as the basis for the tax levy with caps, and the rest of the money would come from the state's general revenue funds.

A *Times Union* story by Paul Vitello described Howard as "a liberal-leaning senator who occasionally takes conservative stands (he is anti-abortion and against increased business taxes) [and who] ran primarily on a record of almost flawless attendance at senate sessions and on a pledge to encourage business to remain in the area."

Proskin took a shot at Howard by pointing out that when Howard gave his lulu to charity, he had declared it on his income tax. Nevertheless, Howard won his second term by nearly eighteen thousand votes (76,357 to 58,504). He ran strongly in Colonie and in Greene County, two Republican strongholds, losing by only four hundred votes in each. "I'm very happy about it," Howard told Michael Muskal of the *Times Union*. "It shows that if you work hard for all of the people, Democrats and Republicans, you can appeal to all of the people in the district."

Joan Motykea, a reporter for the *Times Union*, said that Howard looked exhausted when he was greeted by a standing ovation at his headquarters at the Sheraton Inn on Wolf Road in Colonie. As Howard walked forward to make his victory speech, Motykea reported, "Women kept standing in his path as he made his way through the crowd on his way to the microphone, and they hugged him and kissed him, while the men reached out to grab his hand or pat him on the back." Motykea wrote that one man in the crowd had yelled out, "Next time, it'll be governor."

Maybe down the road. First, Howard decided to run for mayor of Albany in the 1977 Democratic primary against Erastus Corning.

Chapter 9

YOU CAN FIGHT CITY HALL

Howard had ignited a fuse of independence in the Albany County Democratic Party by winning his senate seat in 1974, standing up to Corning on the Fred Ohrenstein issue in 1975, then getting the nomination for senate without Corning's support and winning reelection in 1976. At the age of ninety-one, Dan O'Connell's health was deteriorating, and there were plenty of Democrats who were uncomfortable with Corning taking on even greater power if O'Connell died.

"A lot of people were after me to run for mayor," Howard said. "The people who were traditionally opposed to Corning, the municipal labor unions, had been at constant war with him. Both the police and the firemen unions, too. I was also getting encouraged by a lot of young people who felt they were on their way up in popularity. My friends were encouraging me. And, to be honest, I was also thinking down the pike about running for governor. I was good friends and a great admirer of Governor Hugh Carey. Our sons were great friends. Bob would stay a week with Hugh's son, Kevin, at their summer home on Long Island, and they later roomed together at Le Moyne College."

Regardless, Howard had reservations about running. "I

was up in the air, principally because I had left my first wife at that point. Albany was an Irish Catholic town in those days, and I had deep ties to Albany. I was torn. I did not like the idea of running, and I knew that if I did, right away a lot of people—the 'Corningites'—would bring up my matrimonial situation."

In early January 1977, Howard got a call from his friend Jimmy Ryan, the secretary of the Albany County Democratic Party, who had just visited Dan O'Connell in St. Peter's Hospital. Ryan asked Howard to stop by his house for lunch. When Howard arrived, Ryan told him, "Howard, Dan does not want you to run against Mayor Corning. He's very sincere about that. He'd like you not to run."

Howard replied to Ryan, "You can tell Dan that as long as he's alive, I will not run against Erastus Corning." As Howard later explained, he owed Dan that because he wouldn't have gotten the nomination without him.

When O'Connell died on February 28, Howard declared, "All bets are off." He announced his campaign for the September 8 primary on March 7.

The Hearst newspapers, the morning *Times Union* and the afternoon *Knickerbocker News*, were thrilled with Howard's candidacy. An editorial in the *Times Union* on March 11 read, "We couldn't be happier. Nothing could be healthier for Albany politics than some genuine competition. For more years than most residents have been alive, the Democratic machine has exercised monopoly politics in the city, arrogantly disregarding the public interest. If nothing else, a hard-fought primary by Nolan should put the machine on notice that its cheating ways are going to be challenged not only by those outside the party, but also by bright, energetic people within it."

An editorial in the *Knickerbocker News* on June 2 said, "We are glad to see the Nolan challenge and interpret it as one more sign that this arrogant political machine does not have the power it used to have."

Even the *New York Times* thought Corning's first primary challenge was major news. A March 13, 1977, story was headlined "Albany's Mayor Corning Facing Primary Fight With State Senator." The story began, "A week after the death of Daniel P. O'Connell, Albany's almost legendary Democratic boss, the Democratic machine here received its first challenge in decades when State Senator Howard C. Nolan Jr. announced that he would enter a primary against Mayor Erastus Corning 2nd, the incumbent for 36 years and Mr. O'Connell's heir as county leader."

Reporting from an outdoor news conference in Albany, the *Times* quoted Howard as saying, "No city the size of Albany can be run as a one-man show. It's time we moved into the 20th century." They said Howard pledged to put Albany's government on a "business-like basis" and promised a "wholesale housecleaning" of top officials.

On April 20, Howard blasted Corning at a press conference. As Dennis Nolan's story in the (Troy) *Times Record* recounted, "The city's mayoral race caught fire today when, as expected, challenger and State Senator Howard Nolan accused incumbent Mayor Erastus Corning of 'fiscal ineptitude.' Nolan leveled the charges at a press conference to attack the incumbent administrator's belated discovery that the city owes $1.7 million less than was being reported."

On August 27, the *New York Times* revisited the upstate primary: "Albany's Mayor Is in a Primary Fight, His First in 36 Years in Office." In the *Times* story, Richard Meislin characterized Howard as a "wealthy 44-year-old lawyer" who "has the charisma of a tax accountant but makes up for it through persistence, walking the streets for long hours, ringing doorbells, pumping hands, listening to the gripes of citizens and promising, as politicians do, to solve their problems."

Meislin's characterization of Howard's lack of charisma couldn't have been further off base. "To watch him work a room is something to behold," Howard's brother-in-law, Mike Collins, said. "It was uncanny. If there were fifty people in the room, he knew forty-five of them."

Added Justin Heller, the son of Howard's lifelong friend and partner Mark Heller, "To me, Howard is the kind of person who walked in a room and had stature, magnetism. It's just his honest personality. People are drawn to him. He has that quality. That's part of his success."

Ron Canestrari, who was the mayor of Cohoes for thirteen years and then a New York State assemblyman for twenty-four years, agreed. "Howard had a presence at an event, an aura about him. He had an attraction. He was able to relate to people and it helped his career. He represented the best of a public official. He was caring, a straight shooter, and worked for the people and the common good."

In the *Times* story, Meislin quoted Howard as saying, "Everything here is the same as yesterday. It's pathetic." Meislin also mentioned Howard's campaign posters, which proclaimed, "A city with a future needs a Mayor with a future," a thinly veiled shot at Corning's health concerns at the age of sixty-six as he sought his ninth consecutive term.

Then Meislin wrote that Democratic machine forces, in turn, casually mention to friends in the city's large Irish Roman Catholic constituency that "Mr. Nolan, a Catholic, is living apart from his wife." Howard's worst fear about running had come true—and in the *New York Times*, no less.

"They spread it quietly, from person to person," Howard said. "Albany had this network of wards and committeemen.

They spread that around quickly. Everyone wanted to be friendly with their committeemen and ward leaders. It pissed me off. That was the biggest reason I almost didn't run. I didn't want to get my family involved." His family understood, however. "I've got a good rapport with my kids, still."

Howard could have sunk to the machine's level. "The police and the fire unions were after me to make Corning's relationship with Polly Noonan part of the campaign," he said. "Much to their chagrin, I had no intention of raising that because, to me, I didn't have any intimate knowledge of their relationship other than she was his secretary in the senate. I was just not going to do that. There were enough issues that were out there that should have made me mayor: graft, favoritism to certain contractors."

But Howard's numbers indicated that his message was being ignored, despite what the *Times Union* reported on September 1, a week before the primary. That front-page story of the *Times Union* had blared, "Nolan leads Corning; poll shows." The accompanying story said Howard had a 19 percent lead, but Howard knew those numbers weren't even close.

"It was completely inaccurate," he said. Since his first campaign, Howard had completely trusted his pollster, Dick Barrett. Barrett said that even if Howard had led at one point, it had been by a slim margin, and that his support had faded in recent weeks. "I was never confident in the end that I was going to beat Corning," Howard said.

Here's what Howard was up against. His sister, Mary Beth, was a poll watcher on New Scotland Avenue on primary day. "Helpers would bring in people in wheelchairs and they would go with them into the voting booth," Mary Beth said. "People from the hospital. People from nursing homes."

Mary Beth's husband, Mike Collins, was a poll watcher at St. Catherine's. "He saw this woman standing in the center of the room," Mary Beth said. "She would shake everybody's hand. One time, all these cards she was holding fell to the floor. They were telling them who to vote for. My husband saw that. He ran over to pick up the cards and shouted, 'What do we have here? These are palm cards.' A policeman was there, and he yelled at my husband to stop doing that. He was not happy."

Howard's two-week-older cousin, Tom Nolan, said, "The Albany machine was very powerful. Corning put the pressure on priests and nuns: one last favor. People who liked Howard owed Corning something, and Corning didn't want to give it up yet."

Corning wasn't above bullying people who were supporting Howard to get reelected. After Nebraska Brace, an alderman from Arbor Hill who owned a restaurant and wound up working for Howard, announced his support of Howard, he got a call from the mayor.

Here's an excerpt from Brace's book, *A Man Named Nebraska*[1]:

> Nolan would come to my restaurant almost every other day. Homer Perkins was operating his liquor store across the street. Homer could look out over his front window and observe who was coming and going out of my restaurant. Evidently, he must have called the Mayor and told him Howard Nolan was visiting me an awful lot.

---

[1] Nebraska Brace, *A Man Named Nebraska: A Life Lived in Poverty, Pimping and Politics*. Troy Book Makers, 2006.

The Mayor called me over to his office one day
and says, "I understand that Nolan is coming
in and out of your place every other day."

"That's right. He's my friend."

"Well, I don't like it. I'm a little disturbed about
him coming into your place of business. I really
don't like it."

"Well, I can't help that. He's my friend and he is
at liberty to come into my place as often as he
would like. He's my friend and I'm not going
to give up my friendship with him."

"And you're supporting him, aren't you?"

"I certainly am, Mr. Mayor. I'm supporting
Howard Nolan for mayor."

Corning's face got awful red when I told him
this. He said "You may be excused Nebraska."

When Howard's friend and fellow state senator Carl
McCall accompanied Howard to churches to meet parish-
ioners, he heard from Corning, too. "I got a call from Mayor
Corning," Carl said. "I went to meet with him. He kind of
chewed me out. 'What right do you have to come to Albany,'
he asked, 'and get involved in local politics in Albany?' He
was very unhappy I was working on Howard's campaign. I
thanked him for his advice, but it didn't stop me."

Howard didn't come close to winning. The unofficial
count was 16,472 to 9,402. The only one of fifteen wards that
Howard won was Brace's Third, where he won 90 percent of

the vote. Corning was still mayor for life. But Howard was still a New York State senator, and as the years passed and no other Democrat challenged Corning, who died in office, Howard found solace in his attempt to unseat him.

Chapter 10

CARL

Howard's intransigence in voting for Fred Ohrenstein for New York State Senate minority leader may have ticked off Erastus Corning, but it also helped build a foundation for a deep, ongoing friendship with Carl McCall, another freshman New York State senator in 1975 representing Harlem who also voted for Ohrenstein.

"We changed the Democratic leadership in the state senate," Carl said, a trace of pride still evident more than forty years later.

And Howard, much as he had as a child with his lifelong friend and partner Mark Heller, reached out to Carl. "He did something I thought was surprising," Carl said. "He invited me to his home to have dinner with his first wife. I met his children. We came from very different backgrounds. He came from Albany, and he talked about his practice and how he got into politics. I talked about my experience representing Harlem and Manhattan. I got to know him on a very personal level."

That worked both ways. "We just hit it off," Howard said. "We've been great friends."

Carl, who is currently working full-time as the chairman of

the State University of New York Board of Trustees at the age of eighty-one, was one of five children raised by his mother in the Roxbury section of Boston. Carl's dad left the family and moved to Georgia when Carl was eleven. "My mom was very committed to education to overcome the odds," Carl said.

Carl would spend his life overcoming the odds and eventually becoming the first African American elected to a statewide office in New York as comptroller before he ran for governor in New York. After graduating from Dartmouth with a bachelor of arts degree in government, Carl worked as a high school teacher and bank manager in Boston before joining the army. He opened a church in the Dorchester neighborhood in Boston before moving to New York City, where he quickly became a leader. "I worked with churches in Brooklyn and on voter registration in Harlem," Carl said. "That's how I started in politics."

New York City mayor John Lindsay appointed Carl to head the Commission Against Poverty, and Carl received the backing of Percy Sutton, a prominent Harlem politician, and of David Dinkins, who would become mayor of New York City, as he began his political career. Just like Howard, Carl's first campaign was a successful one to win a seat in the New York State Senate in 1974. After serving two terms in the senate, Carl accepted an appointment from President Jimmy Carter to be a member of the US delegation to the United Nations with the rank of ambassador.

In 1982, Carl lost a bid to be the Democratic candidate for lieutenant governor. Then Governor Mario Cuomo appointed Carl to be the state's commissioner of human rights, a position he held from 1983 to 1984. While working as a vice president for governmental relations with Citicorp (now known as Citibank) from 1985 to 1993, Carl was appointed to the New York City Board of Education and served as its president from 1991 to 1993.

Then he became New York's comptroller, initially in 1993 when he was elected by the state legislature to fill the unexpired term of Republican Edward "Ned" Regan, who resigned on May 7, ending a twenty-five-year-tenure. Carl was elected to the position in 1994 and reelected in 1998 before running unsuccessfully for governor against George Pataki in 2002 after Cuomo's son Andrew, currently the governor of New York, withdrew from the race.

Howard was there all the way, just as Carl was throughout Howard's career. "When I ran for comptroller, he traveled around the state with us," Carl said. "He was right there with me after Ned resigned. A lot of people respected Howard. When I ran for governor, Howard was a major adviser."

Howard served as McCall's campaign manager for the final seven weeks of the campaign, working mostly in New York City. "It's the most work I've done on a campaign since I campaigned against Arnold Proskin in 1976, because Carl is one of my very closest personal friends," Howard told the *Times Union*'s Michael McKeon. "I feel that, domestically, race relations is the biggest single problem facing this country in the next twenty years or so. We have to learn to work together."

Carl appreciated Howard working with him. "He was right there with me until the very end of it," Carl said. And to this day, Carl is grateful for that. "Howard introduced me to people in rural affairs. He took me to the Granger Foundation in Greene County, which was part of his district. I was able to relate to them. We talked about the farmers who produced the food that came to New York City for my people to eat. That was helpful later. Those people remembered me."

Most people did. "Carl has a way of putting people at ease when they first meet him," Howard said.

Both Carl and Howard enjoyed tennis. "We have a lot of fun on the court," Howard told the *Times Union* in a lengthy profile of Carl. "Carl and I are both competitive. We take turns beating each other."

Howard, of course, introduced Carl to horse racing. "He introduced me to Saratoga," Carl said. "He was very knowledgeable in breeding. That became a very important place in the summer for me. We'd go two or three times together."

Howard didn't stop there. "He introduced me to Victor Oberting and Kevin Langan," Carl said. "Howard's friends became my friends." Carl joined the same golf club as Howard, Schuyler Meadows. "He helped me make a lot of connections in Albany, which helped me later."

Along the way, Carl and Howard shared similar values. "We share that we are progressive people," Carl said. "The world we live in now seems to be moving away from that now. People who have greater needs get more help so people can reach their potential."

Faith in people can be tested. Carl and his wife, Dr. Joyce Brown, who became the first female president of the Fashion Institute of Technology in New York, where she still works, were visiting Howard and Shannon in their winter home in Fort Lauderdale. Howard and Carl went out to play tennis two days straight at Coral Ridge County Club, where Howard was a member. "After the second day we played, Howard got a call from the president of the club. He was upset because Howard brought a black man," Carl said. "Howard told the man, 'Carl is a very good friend who happens to be the comptroller of the state of New York. I'll bring whomever I want,' and hung up. I was angry, but I felt good about how Howard handled it. You push back. I felt much better about it, given Howard's reaction."

Howard's brother-in-law, Mike Collins, shared a similar story. "We were at Wolferts Roost Country Club at a party, and Howard and I were at the bar. Joe Frangella, the Republican County chairman, and a couple of thugs came up. Frangella got in Howard's face and raised his voice. Howard was backing an African American to be a member at Wolferts Roost. There were none in Wolferts Roost at the time. Frangella told Howard, 'We don't need people like that in Wolferts Roost.' Howard got up, faced Frangella, and told him calmly to put his face where the sun doesn't shine. He gave it right back to Frangella and said he was a bigot and that there was no reason to keep the African American guy out. Howard didn't yell. Joe said a couple nasty things to Howard's face and walked away. The guy never got in Wolferts Roost."

One time in Paris, Carl and Joyce ran into Howard and Shannon by coincidence. As Carl tells the story, "We were staying with Felix Rohatyn, a famous banker who was credited with bailing New York City out [in 1975] and became the US Ambassador to France [1997–2000]. He invited me to come to talk about the New York State Pension Fund. Howard just happened to be there at the same time."

Rohatyn got Carl and Joyce a reservation at the famous restaurant Le Jules Verne, on the second floor of the Eiffel Tower, more than four hundred feet above ground level. A quick phone call got the reservation switched from two people to four to add the Nolans. When they arrived, the maitre d' said, "Mr. McCall, we have a lovely table for you ... tomorrow night."

After they stopped laughing, the foursome found another restaurant that night. They returned on the following night and dined in the Eiffel Tower. "It was great—a great view," Carl said.

Chapter 11

SHANNON

Shannon Logan has a political pedigree. Born in Lakeland, Florida, Shannon, who is seventeen years younger than Howard, is the daughter of Henry Clayton Logan. A successful citrus grower, consultant, and real estate developer, Logan was elected mayor of Lakeland in 1951. He kept his grove management business headquarters on the second floor of Magnolia Pharmacy in downtown Lakeland. He ran unsuccessfully for the Florida State Senate after serving as Lakeland's mayor. Ironically, Howard was a ten-term state senator in New York who lost in his only try to become mayor of the city of Albany.

Shannon is related by marriage to former Florida governor and US senator Spessard Lindsey Holland and former US congressman James Hardin Peterson. Holland, a conservative Democrat, was governor of Florida from 1941 to 1945 and a US senator from 1946 to 1971. Peterson was a member of the US House of Representatives from 1933 to 1951.

Shannon has three sisters, Shasta, Marcia, and Mary. Shasta is a retired Realtor in Mountain Brook, Alabama, and her husband, Tom Brander, is an IT consultant for the real estate and health care industries. Marcia, who lives in San

Antonio, Texas, authored the book *Frank Goes to Yale*. Her husband, Dan Goodgame, (a former White House correspondent for *Time* magazine), is a vice president for Rackspace. Mary is a legal assistant in Fort Lauderdale, Florida.

Their ninety-five-year-old mother, Ruth McAuley Logan, the daughter of a chemist and a social worker, earned her master's degree in library science after returning to college after Clayton, her husband, died at the age of forty-seven of leukemia. "She has always been beautiful and creative and has artistic ability," Shannon said of her mother. "She designed jewelry, smocked dresses for her girls and their dolls, and put together a nice portfolio of watercolor paintings specializing in animal portraits. Her brother Jim, ninety-seven, is one of the few remaining air force pilots who fought during World War II. My mom fantasized about traveling."

Shannon, who inherited her mother's looks, lived out that fantasy after her mom saw a tiny ad in the *Lakeland Ledger* from Pan American World Airways. Even though she had just completed a bachelor of arts degree in fashion merchandising from Florida State University, Shannon, who had rarely been outside the state of Florida, journeyed to New York for an interview.

At the time, stewardesses had to be at least twenty-one, speak more than one language other than English, and pass an interview offered only once every six months. Shannon's high school French got her past one requirement. She sneaked through another. "Having 20/20 vision without glasses was a must, and mine was 20/400," Shannon said. "Thank God for contact lenses." She was hired in 1971, beginning as a flight attendant and then being promoted to purser in charge of the flight attendants.

"They didn't pay us much, but we had a grand old time," she said. "We did fifteen day trips around the world. It was a hoot. We stayed in five-star hotels. We had access to clubs and parties."

Shannon settled in Manhattan, originally living with two roommates on East Thirty-Sixth Street before getting her own fourth-floor walk-up apartment on Third Avenue between Eightieth and Eighty-First Streets. "It was pretty much a dive, but it was my place," she said. The apartment wasn't far from Central Park, allowing her to walk there with her dachshund, Wilhelm Von Schnapps.

She loved the neighborhood, especially Mrs. Herbst's, a pastry shop that made apple strudel so good that it earned worldwide recognition. Founded by a couple who emigrated from Hungary, Mrs. Herbst's became the supplier for the Hungarian Pavilion at the 1939 World's Fair in New York. In 1947, Mrs. Herbst's moved into an abandoned furniture store on Third Avenue near Eighty-First Street. "They had homemade strudel and the most fantastic hot chocolate with real whipped cream and chocolate shavings to die for," Shannon said. Unfortunately, Mrs. Herbst's closed its doors in 1982, a development that was documented in a *New York Times* story.

During her time with Pan Am, Shannon was featured in three international television commercials for them, which led her to pursue a career as an actress on the side. She worked on two movies, one as a stand-in for Charlotte Rampling, the female lead in Woody Allen's 1980 film, *Stardust Memories*, (about the perils of fame), and the other as an extra on Sylvester Stallone's 1981 film, *Nighthawks*. She saw a great difference in the two filmmakers. "With *Nighthawks*, we'd do one take, and they'd fix it in the editing room," she said. "Woody Allen would wait all day until the sun was just right for the scene we were shooting. Sometimes it would take three takes." The movie industry seemed a little surreal to her, and she thought there was a certain amount of sleaze attached to it. After two years, she had the chance to be in a soap opera but decided to look for a more stable profession.

Soon, the opportunity to go to Iran became available, and the Pan Am crews always welcomed the chance to go to new destinations. So, off she went on a ten-day trip to Teheran. It gave her a chance to learn about the country's artistic culture, about which she had been curious. It was the end of 1979, and the shah had just fallen from power. Shannon had always looked at Iran as a place where the people were handsome and liked Americans. She said, though, that there was a dark side with the way they treated women. She'd watch television and see—after the new regime took over—riots in the streets where acid would be thrown in people's faces, especially women's. "You were supposed to have your arms covered, for example," she said.

To be safe, the flight crews would go out together for dinner. Other ventures were also done in company. "You would go with a friend because it was too dangerous to go alone," she explained.

Other highlights of her Pan Am experience included special assignments. Shannon spent three months in Jakarta, Indonesia, where she worked on HAJ charters, taking people on pilgrimages to Mecca via Pakistan. While there, she studied batik printing on fabric in Bali. She had trips to Paris, Buenos Aires, and Saudi Arabia. Another jaunt was doing White House press charters under the Carter administration, where she met Helen Thomas, the legendary political reporter who worked for UPI for fifty-seven years, as well as Arthur Burns, the head of the Federal Reserve. "There were no TVs on board then," she said. "Few had laptop computers. Sometimes people just wanted to talk. Helen was very nice. She pulled me over one time at the end of a flight and wanted to know if we were happy, if we got enough sleep.

She wanted to know about women in this career. I liked her, because she seemed to care."

Another scenario involved an unexpected incident on a 747 on the tarmac in Narita, near Tokyo one day. As Shannon recalls, "People were boarding, and suddenly, the plane started shaking. I was thrown against a seat. I'm thinking, *They must be loading an elephant in the cargo hold or something.* A passenger told me to look out the window. I did, and was shocked to see that the wings were flapping wildly. We were in an earthquake. The airport was evacuated. We were on the ground for seven hours and then took off on a thirteen-hour flight. I have never been so tired in my life. One customer who worked for a television station videotaped the whole thing with live commentary and managed to send the footage as it happened for the world to see."

Shannon was in Berlin when the wall came down in 1990. "It took a while," she said. "Everybody wanted a piece of the wall. Everybody wanted a piece of history. I wanted a piece of the wall, so I just went over and got a chunk. I still have it. It's not worth anything, because I can't verify its origin, but I know where it's from."

A little bit about Pan Am. According to Shannon, one of the things that made the company special was the fact that they celebrated and embraced diversity. They were proud of the fact that over one hundred and fifty foreign languages were spoken by their collective group of employees over the years. They were truly a global organization, and their trademark, along with Coca Cola's was the most recognized brand in the world at the time. They expected and demanded the best and negotiated everything but quality. The beef they purchased came directly from Kansas. Only the top rated cheeses, wines, foie gras and caviar would do. . . from the source, whether it was from Europe, the Middle East or wherever. They were presumed to be the official flagship carrier of the United States, and they thoroughly enjoyed that perception. Over the top confidence was their mantra, but some would say, maybe this was borderline arrogance. Shannon presented an example of this mindset with the following story:

"It was the inaugural 747 flight to Montevideo, Uraguay from New York (twelve hours). We had been up all night, and after a stop in Buenos Aires, we were crossing the Rio de la Plata on the final leg of our trip. I walked into the cockpit as we started our initial descent to check on things. The pilots were involved in a heated discussion. The captain said, "Oh shit, we don't have permission to land here. The State Department never got the paperwork back to us [the company]." The co-pilot replied, "Well too bad. We have to land; we don't have enough fuel to divert." As I am walking out of the cockpit, I'm thinking, this company that I work for really has some nerve; they are pushing the envelope here. They have taken a risk which might have put us in harm's way. Suddenly, I felt a little anxious, perhaps a fear of the unknown."

She continued, "Nevertheless, our plane landed without incident at the tiny airport. As we taxied to the gate, I looked out the window and was amazed to see a huge crowd on the rooftop of the terminal waving and yelling. Word must have gotten out that we were coming, and they were probably curious to see our new airplane—the Boeing 747SP (special performance). This plane was a shorter version of the popular 747, with only two engines but more powerful than the previous four of it's big brother with a much longer range. This souped-up 747 hot rod—almost the size of a football field—made it's surroundings look like toy structures. Immediately after we stopped, military personnel with machine guns surrounded the aircraft. After the passengers disembarked, our crew was escorted down the ramp stairs into the terminal dining room where the doors were locked. Next, we were invited to enjoy a lavish three hour breakfast while the US ambassador—who had been yanked out of bed at 5:00am—proceeded to negotiate our release. Fortunately, it all worked out well after the dust settled, and we had a nice layover. This ' better to apologize than wait for permission' attitude by our company was cause for concern, though, and ultimately, it would be part of the reason for Pan Am's eventual demise."

It was becoming obvious, with it's financial woes, that Pan Am might not survive. Some of Shannon's friends started going back to school to look for other career opportunities. Shannon followed that path as well. She took a year's leave of absence at one point and worked as an administrative assistant for Jeremy Lang and Associates—an architectural firm in Manhattan off Fifth Avenue—for six months, to see if she wanted to become an architect. Lang had apprenticed under the celebrated Robert Stern. Then she switched directions and spent the next six months working for David Bell Associates, an agent for five European companies that printed designs on fabrics for upholstering.

In the winter of 1985, the same year Shannon received a master of science degree in architectural interior design from Pratt Institute in Brooklyn, Howard walked into her life.

Shannon's friend Aimee Bratt, like Shannon a purser with Pan Am, who later wrote *Glamour and Turbulence: I Remember Pan Am, 1966–91*, had been trying to arrange a double date so Shannon could meet Howard. After a couple of unsuccessful tries, Aimee gave Shannon's number to Howard. He called her and asked her out for a drink at the Metropolitan Club, a social club in New York City founded by J. P. Morgan to which Howard belonged. Howard still lived in Albany, but he spent plenty of time in Manhattan.

It's hard to say who had lower expectations on their first date, Howard or Shannon. As he explains, "I'd been legally separated from Gerrie for nearly ten years, and I had no intention of getting married again." Shannon agreed to meet Howard for a drink, but she had a backup plan to fake a later commitment that evening if needed.

Shannon was prepared for her initial encounter with Howard. "I had on a sexy little Calvin Klein number that I liked a lot and that looked good on me." Howard had double-parked his car and was waiting for her inside the building. "There he was," Shannon said. "He looked like a professor. Tweed jacket. Ruffled hair."

Shannon told herself, "Don't start judging," but she did anyway—when Howard walked her into the Metropolitan Club. "It was a private club, which was beautiful, with a formal dining room overlooking Central Park. Older male professional waiters. I was impressed with the place, and we had a great conversation. I was confident. I was well informed and educated. I had choices. I was looking for a relationship."

Then Howard asked her where she wanted to be in five years. "Why did he bring that up? That was a big gamble," Shannon says now. But that evening she told Howard, "I want to be married and have a child, in that order." She continued, "And if you're not in the same frame of mind, don't waste my time. If you don't think I'm the right person, don't lead me on."

Howard took it all in stride, which impressed Shannon. "He wasn't taken aback at all. He was very easy to talk to. Maybe he wanted a relationship, too."

When Howard asked Shannon to stay and have dinner with him, she told him, "I have to make a phone call to see if I can get out of an earlier commitment." Then she walked off, made an imaginary phone call, returned to the table, and agreed to dinner. Howard smiled. "I think he probably knew," Shannon explains.

They began dating. Then Howard found out that Shannon was assigned to a flight to Paris with Pan Am. That time, Howard upped the ante. "He bought a ticket full fare and went with me, a $1,200 round-trip," Shannon said. "That got my attention."

Howard could afford it. "It was a lot of money, but fortunately I had made a lot of money before I got into the senate through real estate," he said. "Money wasn't really an issue."

Still, Shannon remembers a visit by Mark Heller years later when they talked about the airfare. "It blew Mark away, because Howard is so frugal," Shannon said. Mark told her, "Howard must have liked you a lot."

The Pan Am crew members traveling with Shannon were impressed. "My guy was on the plane," Shannon said, "and they thought it was great." Pat Palermo, the purser in first class, moved Howard up to first class. "They were obviously smitten with each other," said Palermo thirty years later, now working as a vice president for Corcoran Real Estate in New York City. "Shannon was very professional and trying to keep it together, and Howard was such a gentleman. I had a couple of seats in first class. I had her walk up to him with a glass of champagne and had him escorted to first class. Then we invited him to ride with us on the crew bus, so he came along to the hotel, too. It was history after that. How much more romantic could it have been?"

Howard found a way. He told Shannon he wanted to buy her a dress. "I said, 'If he wants to buy me one, I'm not going to refuse it,'" Shannon said. "I took him into the Yves St. Laurent store on the Rue du Faubourg Saint-Honore. The prices were five hundred dollars a dress. I was thinking, *Is he going to blink?* We didn't find anything we liked. However, at the second place, Ungaro, I found a classic dress that I ended up wearing for years. Howard took me to Le Souffle, a restaurant specializing in souffles, and we had a great time. Then we started seeing each other. He took me into the senate chambers and introduced me to everyone. We started going to parties and did a lot of traveling. Howard liked to travel. When I met him, he was ready to have fun. After we married, we were on a mission to see the world—a lifelong dream."

Shannon discovered many qualities that she admired in Howard. "One thing about Howard, he's very good under pressure," she said. "If we have to make a flight, he times it to the last second. It's fourth and one. He's going to make it. One reason I was so attracted to him was that he had this laser-like ambition and focus. Something I liked from the beginning was that he was a self-made man. He was taught at a very early age that you have to work for what you get and you have responsibilities."

For a long while, their relationship involved commuting between Albany and Manhattan. Eventually she told Howard that she needed more. She told him she was thinking about leaving, going to Arizona. "We were two years into our relationship," Shannon said, "and we were stagnant. It was a matter of pushing the envelope a little bit."

As a Catholic, the idea of divorce horrified Howard, but he knew it was time. "He got divorced within the next year," Shannon said. A year later, they were married on November 26, 1988. She's been trying to keep up ever since. "We've had a good run," she said.

Howard would eventually retire from the senate (1994) and his law firm (1997). Shannon kept working with Pan Am until it went out of business in 1991. Delta, American, and

United (airlines) would acquire Pan Am's routes and hire many of their employees. Shannon worked for Delta for a while and then retired from the airline industry. It was time. After all, in 1989, she had started her own company, SLN Associates, designing commercial interiors. She worked with a decorator, Mary Tracy. Mary would do the colors and materials, and Shannon did the space planning. "It was all done by hand," Shannon said, "very time consuming." Back then, in the 1980s, only 10 percent of architectural firms were using computers as a design tool. When Mary died—we miss her; she was so talented and a wonderful human being—the company folded in 2009. Finally, Shannon studied art appraisal at New York University and received a two-year certificate. She has continued her interest in this field and is still involved in it to this day.

Thanks to Carl McCall, Shannon got to meet Hillary Clinton when her husband was president. "I've been a very big fan of hers," Shannon said. "Carl had tickets for one of her speeches in Washington. He didn't particularly want to go, so I went to the speech in mid-August. I shook her hand. She's little. I'm five feet six, and she's maybe five feet four. Her hands are like velvet. I'll bet she's never picked up a hammer in her whole life. As I shook her hand, I told her, 'Carl McCall says hello.' She smiled."

Later in August, after a day at Saratoga Race Course, Howard and Shannon dined with Carl and Joyce, his wife, at the Wishing Well, an incredibly popular restaurant just a few miles north of Saratoga Springs. As Shannon tells the story, "We were having dinner together, and Carl said, 'Hillary called me up and invited my wife and me to the White House.' Joyce thought that was great." Shortly afterward, Hillary won a seat in the US Senate representing New York.

With extra time on their hands, Shannon and Howard

started traveling more. Those years made up some of their best memories together. "We went to France a lot, mostly to Paris," Shannon said. "We'd take two weeks off and rent a car. Hit the castles. Go to where the D-Day invasion happened in Normandy. Go watch horse racing in Deauville. We walked around the cities and got to know them like the backs of our hands. We went to Rome a lot. It was great."

Chapter 12

TERM AFTER TERM

With stunning consistency, Howard won election after election from 1978 through 1992. In his last eight elections, Howard had more votes on a major party line than any other senator.

In 1978, Mayor Corning backed Carmen Chang, who ran in a primary against Howard for his senate seat. Howard won easily and afterward received a call from Corning. They met in Corning's office. "He told me, 'I think it's time we had peace,'" Howard said, and Howard was happy to agree.

That November, against Bob Prentiss, Howard won re-election with 63.11 percent of the vote, much higher than his winning percentages in 1974 (50.71) and 1976 (57.63). He would win his seven subsequent terms with more than 63 percent of the vote.

In 1980, Howard defeated popular, civic-minded Mary Dumas, who had been appointed to the Private Industry Council by Corning in 1977. Three years later, she took on Howard. He won 67.55 percent of the vote, including a surprising victory in the Republican-dominated town of Bethlehem, which hadn't elected a local Democrat in its 188-year history. Asked how he did it by *Times Union* reporter

Alan Fram, Howard said, "I don't know. Sometimes you just get lucky." Dumas subsequently won the YWCA's Tribute to Women Award in 1986.

On January 7, 1981, a *Times Union* story by Alan Miller detailed Howard hiring his longtime friend and political ally John "Jack" McNulty to be his legislative aide specializing in criminal justice and local government. McNulty, whose dad served as Albany County sheriff in the 1930s, had resigned from his second term as sheriff in February 1979 after a confrontation with the Democratic-controlled Albany County Legislature over overtime for jail workers.

"It's well known that Jack McNulty and I have always been close politically and personally," Howard told Miller. "He's a very, very valuable addition to my staff. I've always been impressed with his knowledge."

Getting hired by Howard allowed McNulty to work in the county legislature with his son Michael, who would go on to become a US congressman. Michael was working as assistant director to the legislature's administrative registrations review committee.

Miller wrote that Howard's addition of Jack McNulty "unites in one office two maverick Democrats who independently challenged Albany Mayor and County Democratic Chief Erastus Corning." Jack McNulty had defeated a Democratic machine candidate in a primary on the way to being elected sheriff in 1973.

Michael McNulty said, "My dad was the first to run in a primary for sheriff. Understandably, his supporters were few and far between, but one of them was Howard. Howard endorsed Dad, Dad won, and the rest is history. People elected my dad against overwhelming odds. When I decided to run for the assembly in '82, I didn't have the support of the party either. We all have a history of independence from the party."

Maverick or not, Howard thanked those Democrats, Republicans, and Independents who voted for him in an ad in the *Times Union*, in which he promised to work hard and represent all the people in the district. "To those who contributed so much to the success of my campaign, my very deep gratitude and appreciation. Very Sincerely, Howard C. Nolan Jr., New York State Senator-Elect." At the bottom of the ad was the slogan "His special interest is people!"

On January 8, 1981, *Times Union* reporter Alan Fram covered a speech that Howard made to members of the Republican-leaning Bethlehem Chamber of Commerce at the Albany Motor Inn. "Nolan called for business tax cuts and a rolling back of government regulations which interfere with business. His speech was a big hit." Fram quoted Bethlehem Chamber of Commerce President Edward Panner II: "Initially, I was a little concerned about the reception he'd get here, but he was just excellent."

In early July 1981, Howard managed to get involved in a controversy from his hospital bed at St. Peter's, where he'd gone for hernia surgery. At the time, a much-debated sales tax law, which would increase sales tax in New York City to subsidize mass transit, came up for a vote as the senate rushed to adjournment for the summer. Howard was opposed to the increase, but he had to miss the vote.

"It's becoming the world's most famous hernia," Howard told *Knickerbocker News* columnist E. J. McMahon Jr. He told McMahon he had alerted Fred Ohrenstein, the man he had helped become Democratic minority leader, about his impending surgery and absence. "I told him, 'Fred, you wouldn't want me there anyway.' Fred affirmatively said, 'I'll have you marked excused.'" Nevertheless, because he was absent, Howard's vote was automatically cast in favor of the sales tax legislation, which passed. That led to a court decision throwing out the legislation.

Ohrenstein, who had supported the increase, told McMahon he hadn't told the clerk about Howard's absence because he thought Howard himself had asked the clerk to be excused. Howard spoke with Ohrenstein about the matter and told McMahon, "It was a misunderstanding."

In the *Knickerbocker News*, though, McMahon pointed out a concern about Howard: "Sources say the many-faceted Albany Democrat—whose private business interests include horse breeding, restaurants, and real estate, not to mention his Albany law firm—doesn't spend that much time in the senate chamber. Nolan flatly denies any implication he isn't devoting enough time to his job. His official attendance record is nearly perfect with no absences and only a handful of excusals recorded in the last seven years."

Regardless, Howard's law firm and his real estate dealings continued to prosper. Howard and his partner, Norris MacFarland, operating as HMC Associates, bought the seventeen-acre Delaware Plaza just south of Albany in 1973. Howard still owns that plaza and the one in Plattsburgh in upper northeast New York State, both with partners.

Howard's four-year truce with Corning was tested when he was offered a job as Ed Koch's upstate campaign manager. Koch was running against Mario Cuomo, whom Corning had backed, in the 1982 Democratic primary for governor. "I met Koch and liked him, but I wanted to ask Corning about it," Howard said. "Corning had already endorsed Cuomo. Corning said it would appear to others in the Democratic Party that we were at war again. I thought about it for a couple of days and then told him, 'Mayor, as usual, you're very perceptive. I'm not going to do it.'"

Howard won reelection in 1982 in a landslide, beating

James Sheehan 90,204 to 33,119 with the highest percentage of his ten victories, 72.13.

In 1984, Howard took on Joseph Frangella, who had been the Albany County Republican Party chairman for ten years. In extensive, adjoining articles about each candidate in the *Albany Student Press* on October 23, Howard shared his views on a multitude of topics germane to college students:

- He had voted in 1983 for a bill to kill tuition increases for State University of New York schools, including Albany State, now known as the University of Albany.
- He had cosponsored a bill in the state senate to raise the drinking age in the state from nineteen to twenty-one. He called drunk-driver statistics "staggering" and also disclosed that the subject was debated frequently at his home. At the time, his seven children were aged sixteen to twenty-three. He said he agreed with his kids that not all nineteen- and twenty-year-olds abuse alcohol, but said, "Unfortunately a lot of people have to pay for the sins of a few." The 1984 National Minimum Drinking Age Act reduced federal highway funding by 10 percent for any state with drinking minimums under twenty-one years old, and New York got in line, raising the minimum age from nineteen to twenty-one effective December 1, 1985.
- He supported both a state and a federal Equal Rights Amendment to mandate equal pay for women.
- He also wanted SUNY schools to be allowed to upgrade their sports programs to Division I, which did happen years later.

Frangella took a couple of shots at Howard in the article for his senate phone bills. He said he didn't care that Howard's phone bill was below the average of state senators.

"The issue is not what other senators are doing, it's what he's doing." As Howard explained, "Greene County was part of my district, and every call to that county was long distance."

Frangella also said he wouldn't accept per diem payments if elected, as Howard did. That statement, however, contradicted an article in the *Times Union* on October 14 in which Frangella had said that he would accept per diem payments.

Frangella ran TV commercials proclaiming "Shame on you, Howard Nolan," but Howard crushed Frangella, capturing 63.15 percent of the vote. "That was one election that I felt personally so good about," Howard said.

Two years later, Howard ran against a young lawyer named Peter Crummey, who worked for the town of Colonie and was running for political office for the first time in his life. Ironically, Howard had been close friends with Crummey's wife's parents, Mike and Carol, since high school. "I had gotten Peter's father a job with the state," Howard said, "and then his son ran against me."

Howard, now fifty-four, was ensconced in the senate, sitting on three of its most important committees: Rules, Finance, and Codes. The *Spotlight* published abutting articles on the two candidates, both written by Tom McPheeters, on October 22, 1986. "Our job, constitutionally, is to enact laws," Howard told McPheeters. "Practically, though, what has evolved is that the state legislature has become an ombudsman for the people we represent." As an example, Howard touted the Port of Albany, which had received more than $25 million in state funds in the previous decade.

McPheeters wrote, "To combat charges of absenteeism from the senate, [Nolan] presented a three-color chart showing he was marked present in 94, 97, and 96 percent of votes over the past three years."

Crummey, who had a thirty-page booklet explaining his

policy positions, said of Howard, "He's been talking about the Port of Albany since the 1982 election. I wonder how long he's going to live off that. It had nothing to do with Howard Nolan. It just happened to be in his district." Crummey added that Howard "has done a tremendous amount for himself. The folks in this town know that."

Regarding Howard's alleged absenteeism, Crummey had a cardboard cutout of the allegedly absent Howard that he called Crummey's Dummy. Crummey said of Howard, "It's the arrogance he's developed over the years. He's not productive at all."

Two weeks later, Howard produced another victory, taking 66.95 percent of the vote. Howard's total of 73,349 votes was more than double Crummey's 36,206. On December 1, 1987, the *New York Times* published a provocative opinion piece by Howard under the headline "Make New York Legislature Truly Part-Time or Truly Full-Time":

> As a seventh-term state senator who has become increasingly concerned with the direction in which the New York State Legislature is moving, I believe we have come to a critical juncture in our state's history. Given the enormous growth in the length of the legislative sessions, the corresponding increase in lawmaker salaries and the creation of more and more positions offering extra stipends or "lulus," I think it is time to let New York's citizens decide whether the State Legislature is to be in practice, as well as in theory, a part-time government entity or whether it should ultimately function as a truly full-time legislative body.

Howard went on to say that he was planning, as a first

step, to introduce a constitutional amendment that would, if passed by the legislature, put this question directly to the voters. He said his amendment would limit the length of the legislative session to three months, down from an average of six months, and permit the governor—pursuant to a two-thirds vote by the senate and assembly—to call the legislature back to the capital should an issue arise requiring immediate legislative action.

Howard continued, "Part-time legislators should receive part-time compensation—between $10,000 and $20,000. By limiting the session and reducing legislative salaries, lawmakers would be free to serve the public and make a living outside politics, and, accordingly, be free from dependence on their legislative jobs for their livelihood. This could reduce the likelihood of vulnerability to the demands of special interest groups who now play such a major role in re-election campaigns.

"While I am opposed to the concept of a full-time, professional legislature," Howard concluded, "I believe it should be up to New York's citizens to make the final decision."

Remarkably, more than two decades after Howard's proposal, another New York City newspaper, the *New York Sun*, referenced Howard's piece in an editorial on May 29, 2008: "A former state senator, Howard C. Nolan, was on to something twenty years ago when he proposed a constitutional amendment that would limit the length of the legislative session to three months." The story quoted the reduced compensation Howard proposed and the effect it might have on special interest groups. "I never saw that follow-up article," Howard said. "That's amazing."

In 1988, Howard won reelection with 69.37 percent of the vote, defeating G. Scott Morgan.

At the end of 1989, Howard lost a friend and one of his

longtime political backers, multi-decorated marine war hero Andy Anderson, who had publicly supported Howard in his battles with Mayor Erastus Corning. In a 1975 *Knickerbocker News* story, Anderson, then the Guilderland Town Democratic chairman, had said that he backed Howard "out of a sense of loyalty and friendship. If a man cannot stand with his friend in the heat of battle, then the definition of friendship and loyalty must be reviewed."

A native of Cranston, Rhode Island, Anderson served in the Marine Corps from 1953 to 1973. Serving two tours of duty in Vietnam, he was wounded in his left eye while directing the recovery of two downed airmen in a mission behind enemy lines. He was awarded the Bronze Star, the Silver Star, the Legion of Merit, the Vietnamese Gallantry Cross, and the Purple Heart. He was also extremely active in the Cerebral Palsy Center for the Disabled, where Howard served for forty years.

Anderson was only fifty-eight when he was stricken with a heart attack and died in St. Peter's Hospital on December 30, 1989. Howard said of his friend,

> He was smart, loyal, and a very hard worker. He was a marine, which touched me. I can't say enough good things about him. I met Andy Anderson when he was in charge of the Marine Corps Reserve in Albany. We became friends and he was very active in the Democratic Party. Andy was an unbelievably good human being. When he retired from the Marines Corps, he became a vice president of Bankers Trust in Albany. Then he was nominated for a new office, Albany County executive. The nominating meeting was on a Thursday night, as usual. Apparently, Mayor Corning was very upset

that Anderson was going to be nominated because Anderson was close to me. Supposedly, Corning had met with Dan O'Connell and told him he was going to retire if Andy was nominated. That's how Jim Coyne got nominated. He won, and then he won reelection by a larger margin. Jim's hands were tied almost from day one by the Albany County Legislature. Jim hired Nolan and Heller to win a lawsuit against the Albany County Legislature, in effect a test of power between the county executive and the legislature. And we won the case. Corning had Jim come over and, after that, they had a working relationship.

Seeking his ninth term against Republican Mark Stuart later in 1990, Howard was backed by the *Times Union*. Citing Howard's vision of the future, the newspaper declared its endorsement:

Of all the candidates, Senator Nolan is almost alone in alerting constituents to the need for improved racial relations. In a melting pot state like New York, that objective should be high on every candidate's list of priorities. Not surprisingly, Senator Nolan's strong palliatives for legislative reform have gone unheeded in a house controlled by the opposition. By sending him back to the Senate for a ninth term, voters can send a message that they, too, want a change in the way the Legislature does business. Sen. Nolan wins our endorsement as a lawmaker who throughout his tenure had demonstrated constructive leadership.

Howard won in 1990, taking 67.22 percent of the vote.

In 1991, Howard made a bid for Albany County Democratic chairman, but he failed to unseat Harold Joyce. A year later, Howard won his tenth consecutive term, taking 67.06 percent of the vote against Daniel Ehring. His final senate term would end in 1994.

Howard's friend Marcia Aronowitz, said, "In Howard's twenty years in the senate, we were never embarrassed by him. There wasn't a moment where we thought he did the wrong thing. And you can't say that about too many of them."

Chapter 13

BLUE SKY

Howard seldom acted on impulse when contemplating a major decision. With his lifelong love of Thoroughbreds jump-started by legislation that established the New York Thoroughbred Breeding and Development Fund to improve breeding and racing Thoroughbreds in New York, he finally confronted his deep passion for Thoroughbreds. He needed to decide whether to get involved in an investment that he knew was extremely risky.

"I'd been thinking about it for several years," Howard said. "I was starting to become successful through my law office and real estate ventures, and I had some money lying around that I wasn't doing anything with. So I went and read the legislation, and that persuaded me to get into the New York breeding program."

He was doing his homework. Actually, Howard had been doing his homework for years. "I had followed racing ever since I went to my first Saratoga Sale when I was eighteen. I stayed a fan. I went to the races a lot at Saratoga. I read vociferously about horses. I had a good background. I did know a lot about the industry."

What Howard didn't know at the time was that the New

York breeding program would evolve into the best incentive program in the United States for breeders, owners, and horsemen. Along the way, New York–breds would become good enough to win Grade 1 stakes in open competition. Funny Cide, for example, would win the Kentucky Derby.

Howard targeted the 1976 Saratoga Yearling Sale in August—and he did more homework. "I had gotten a catalog. I had decided that I might buy a horse. I took it with me over to Cape Cod. I went through the catalog on the beach, and I identified that if I bought a horse, it was going to be a filly. If I was going to get involved, I wanted to get involved in the breeding."

He didn't have much choice. Public officials in New York were allowed to breed and own horses, but not to race them in New York because of a scandal in the 1930s.

Howard set a lofty goal, to breed the winners of the two most prestigious mile-and-a-half stakes in the world— the Belmont Stakes, the final leg of the Triple Crown, and Europe's greatest race, the Prix de l'Arc de Triomphe. "Not necessarily with the same horse," Howard said.

Howard had visited a Standardbred farm in Orange County near Goshen, New York, and met the owners, Ben and Steve Ostrer. "I became friendly with them, in particular with Ben, who was the hands-on guy. Ben really ran the farm. They had a couple of stallions. They had a farm manager by the name of Tom Smith. I got friendly with Tom Smith. I called up Ben and asked him if he would let his farm manager help me buy a yearling, someone who knew about conformation—the physical aspects—of a yearling."

In July 1976, a month before the Saratoga Yearling Sale, Howard committed to buying a yearling. He bought his first horse, a yearling filly, for $20,000, and named her Karen's Lady for his youngest daughter. "She was a nice-looking filly, but it turned out she had a throat problem," Howard said. The closest she came to winning a race was a distant sixth in her debut, the first of eight unproductive starts. "I kept her as a broodmare and eventually sold her in foal to Singh for $250,000 at Keeneland," Howard said. "The reason she had become so valuable was because of her younger half-brother, Noble Nashua, who was a multiple graded stakes winner. So I had a filly I had bought for $20,000 who didn't race well, but I made a lot of money from selling her as a broodmare in foal a couple of years later."

A week later, in the Fasig-Tipton Sale for Horses of Racing Age at Saratoga, Howard bought two unraced three-year-old fillies, Belle de Jour for $3,500 and Crafty Wind for $2,500. Howard asked Smith to recommend a good trainer outside of New York, and Smith suggested Jimmy Hausweld. "He was training at Keystone in Philadelphia," Howard said. "I sent both three-year-olds to him. The fillies were getting close to a race, and he called me up one day and said they both had worked. Belle de Jour went in :49 or something [for four furlongs, a half-mile]. Hausweld told me, 'The other one couldn't beat me in a race.' He suggested I retire her to become a broodmare." Belle de Jour won just one of ten starts and earned $3,163. "Hausweld recommended that I retire her to become a broodmare, too, so that's what I did," Howard said.

He was not emotionally attached to either filly. "I've always looked at it as a business that I love. I've never fallen in love with a horse. You have to make sure you treat it as a business, because if you don't, it will eat you up financially."

Howard's friend Jim Patrick, who owned Bumstead Chevrolet in Troy and was also on the board of the Cerebral Palsy Center while Howard was chairman, owned and lived on a farm outside of Troy. "When I was talking to him about the horses, he made a suggestion to me that he had just bought a share in Giacometti, a stallion from England standing at Gainesway Farm in Lexington. Giacometti had placed in all three Triple Crown races in England: second in the 2,000 Guineas, third in the Epsom Derby, and second in the St. Leger in 1974. He suggested, 'Why don't we become partners and breed the two fillies to Giacometti and put them in a sale in November?' He was going to board the horses on his farm. They got in the November sale at Keeneland, where Belle de Jour brought $38,000 and Crafty Wind got $16,000."

Belle de Jour would have gotten Howard close to his breeding goal, for she would foal 1985 Kentucky Derby winner Spend A Buck, the 1985 Horse of the Year and Champion Three-Year-Old. "I was very happy that I was intelligent enough to buy the dam of a Kentucky Derby winner in my lifetime, even though I sold her," Howard said. "I felt great."

In 1977 Howard cemented his long-term involvement in Thoroughbred breeding by purchasing a farm outside of Goshen, twenty miles from Ben and Steve Ostrer's farm. "It was fifty-five acres and it included a track," he said. "It had an old house built in 1780—a big colonial house—and two barns, a pasture, a track, and extra land, which was a paddock." He named it Blue Sky Farm. "I don't know why. I just like catchy phrases."

Howard leased 125 acres next to the farm. "Then I proceeded to hire Tom Smith," he said. "I talked to Ben, who had no problem with it. Tom was spending more and more time at my farm, and Ben really didn't need a farm manager."

Howard wasn't done. "Six months after I bought the farm, the old farmer next to me, who had a three-hundred-acre farm, died. He was a widower with two sons, both grown. One lived in California and the other in Arizona. They put this farm up for sale, and I called the broker and made an offer to buy it. He pooh-poohed me, because he thought it was worth a lot more. But a year later, the For Sale sign was still there. The broker called me up and asked if I was still interested. I told him that I was, but at the same price I had offered the year before. The broker told me, 'I'll get back to you tomorrow.' The guy called me back the next day and said we had a deal. I drew up a contract at the price I had offered, and we ended up buying it."

Howard journeyed to Maryland twice to purchase more broodmares and one stallion in private sales for his now sizable farm. The stallion he bought was Quick Card, a winner of ten of twenty-seven starts who earned $209,633, most of it under the care of Hall of Fame trainer Tom "T. J." Kelly.

"As a stallion, Quick Card was a disaster," Howard said. "The first year, I bred him to forty mares, which was a big number in those days. I stood Quick Card for five years. I started him off at $4,000 (as a stallion fee). His book (the number of mares he served) diminished each year. He never sired a black-type horse (stakes winner.) I finally sold him to some people in Minnesota for not much money. I did sell a yearling by him at Ocala one time in his first or second crop for six figures."

Before Howard sold him, Quick Card returned to the races. After Tom Smith had a heart attack and retired, Howard hired John Pucek as farm manager. Quick Card was standing stud at the time. "At some point, Pucek says to me, 'I watch Quick Card running out in the field and I think he's sound and we might consider putting him back in training,'" Howard said. "It made sense to me. We had a track and riders who were breaking horses. So we put him back in training, and he was training well. I sent Pucek and his wife to Saratoga to train him there."

Howard went up to Saratoga unannounced one morning and was surprised. "The horse was in the stall, and I couldn't find Pucek. It was late morning, and he was still sleeping. A groom said he hadn't been there that morning, so I fired him."

Howard found a new trainer, Ralph Sanseverino, and Quick Card continued to train well. On September 8, 1978, Quick Card returned at Belmont Park, under new ownership, for his first start in more than eleven months in an allowance race. Unfortunately, Tiller, a multiple stakes winner, was in the race. "Tiller was coming off a layoff, but he was obviously the horse to beat," Howard said. "Tiller got the lead inside the sixteenth pole, and Quick Card, who was last or next to last, finished third by a neck. He was going right past Tiller after the finish line."

Unfortunately for Howard, Quick Card never raced well again, finishing ninth, seventh, and eighth twice before he was re-retired.

"T. J. Kelly wasn't happy with me," Howard explained, "He called me up and said, 'Why is he being raced? I sold him as a stallion prospect.'

"You didn't say he couldn't be raced," Howard said. We made up our friendship, however, and later, two of his sons, Larry and Pat, trained for me."

Howard said Quick Card's failed stallion career had a substantial effect on his future breeding decisions. "It influenced me considerably. I came to the conclusion that there weren't any good turf stallions who had raced only in the United States. Europe is a different story. I never bred to a turf horse or stood a stallion who raced just in the United States."

Regal Embrace certainly fit the bill. He never raced in the United States. Bred by E. P. Taylor and racing for famed Windfields Farm, Regal Embrace, a huge horse who measured seventeen hands[2] tall made all of his eleven starts in Canada. Unraced at two, Regal Embrace won the 1978 Queen's Plate, Canada's most prestigious race for three-year-olds, equaling the stakes record set by Victoria Park in 1960. Regal Embrace finished his career with seven wins, two seconds by a head, a fourth, and a fifth in eleven starts.

"Joe Thomas of Windfield Farms called me and told me they had heard good things about Blue Sky and wanted to stand Regal Embrace in New York," Howard said. He made a deal to stand him at Blue Sky with an option to purchase him. Windfield sent a dozen mares to him, and Howard bought him and syndicated him. "He turned out to be a good sire in New York."

Another of Howard's clients at Blue Sky was Sonny Werblin, owner of the New York Jets, chairman of Madison Square Garden, and builder and manager of the Meadowlands Sports Complex. "Werblin called me out of the blue," Howard said. "The reason he called was that his best friend, David Yunich, the CEO and chairman of the board of Macy's, had a brother who was a doctor in Albany. His brother's partner, Dr. Nate Fradkin, lived next door to me."

At the time, Werblin had all his horses in New Jersey. "He had decided to go to New York because of the New York–bred program," Howard said. "That's how I wound up with Sonny Werblin as a client. He sent his stallion, PR Man, who was a good racehorse, and all his other breeding stock to Blue Sky Farm. I got to know him, and he was a terrific guy. He invited me to Knicks games, and he insisted I sit with him, front row courtside."

Howard also had a great relationship with Mike Flynn, who worked for Howard for twenty years before taking a job, with Howard's backing, as executive director of the New

---

[2] A hand is approximately four inches.

York Thoroughbred Breeders. "As a hands-on horsemen, there weren't many better than Mike Flynn," Howard said. Howard rewarded Flynn by giving him a piece of Blue Sky Farm after he sold it in Goshen in 1986 and restarted it at a converted dairy farm he had purchased in Fort Edward.

Two years later, Howard's announcement that he was selling Blue Sky Farm and auctioning off his 160 horses and stallion shares in Filiberto, King Pellinore, and Instrument Landing created headlines. In one story, he said he was working 120 hours a week. "I don't want to work 220 hours," he said. "I'm directly involved in the breeding, buying, and selling of horses. That takes time, and I don't have the time."

Howard sold the farm and divested almost all his horses, keeping a remaining handful with Gus Schoenborn on his farm in Coxsackie. Then he reengaged:

> Gus got me involved in buying Comet Shine, a two-year-old champion in Canada. We stood him at Gus's farm for several years. He wasn't a top stallion, but we made money with him. Then he called me one day a few years later. He wanted to get me involved with Rodeo, a brilliantly fast colt who had gotten hurt as a three-year-old. Robbie Davis rode that horse and told me many times he was the fastest horse he ever rode. We bought him and stood him at stud at Gus's farm. I initially bought 40 or 50 percent of him, then sold off some shares, which made a lot of money. His trainer, Stan Hough, a very good horseman and a very nice guy, brokered the deal.

Then Shannon and I decided that we should buy a farm. I had a friend, Bert Freed, who owned Flah's with his wife,

Barbara. Bert had gotten into real estate where he lived in Columbia County. I called him up one day and we finally bought a 135-acre farm in Nassau, New York, that had two houses on the property in 1998. I started Blue Sky Farm for the third time. It was a former dairy farm. I built that into a Thoroughbred farm. I must have owned it for four years. In four years, I went through three farm managers. We sold it at the end of 2001.

Then we went back to buying horses. We sold a few of them and we moved our seven or eight broodmares to Kentucky. We wanted to get out of the New York program, which was going downhill. Then it got resurrected by the casino at Aqueduct. When they finally passed the legislation for the casino, I moved them back to New York. By that time, Gus had sold his farm and I talked to Joe McMahon (who operates McMahon of Saratoga Thoroughbreds). And he didn't have any room. I was in a hurry to qualify to get them to New York for the breeding program. He recommended two sisters who owned H and H Farm, outside of Fort Edward. I boarded my horses there; then I moved them to Clermont Farm in Germantown. Now most of them are at Joe McMahon's. He had bought another farm and had more room. I probably still have forty horses. I'm buying and selling them all the time. I hope within the next year or two to get down to five or six broodmares.

Broodmares will produce foals that Howard can sell at auction or keep to race to remain in the game he's always loved.

Howard and his sister, Mary Beth

Howard and lifelong friend Father Peter Young
(Courtesy NYS Senate)

Albany Mayor Erastus Corning and Howard
(Courtesy NYS Senate)

Margaret and Fred Martin and Howard

Howard's senate staff in later years (left to right): Dwayne Williams (intern), Barbara Jensen, Barbara Zwack Ardman, Nebraska Brace, Howard (front), Chris Gifford, Michael Flynn, Nona Teabout, Charlie Gaddy, and Pat McCarville. Missing Larry King (Credit NYS Senate)

Comptroller H. Carl McCall and Dr. Joyce Brown

Lt. Gov. MaryAnn Krupsak, Gov. Hugh Carey, and Howard

*Sheriff Jack McNulty, Howard, Assemblyman Dick Conners,
and US Rep. Mike McNulty (Courtesy NYS Senate)*

*The Wildensteins, Bailey, Fabre, and Nolans in the winner's
circle in 1993 at the Breeders' Cup Classic
(Credit Skip Dickstein)*

Arcangues with Bailey and Fabre (Credit Shyeki Kikkawa)

Hy Rosen cartoon (Courtesy the Times Union)

134

Howard and Shannon Nolan after the surprise win
(Credit Kathy Nolan)

Chapter 14

THE FRENCH CONNECTION

In 1993, Arcangues won the $3 million Breeders' Cup Classic by two lengths under Jerry Bailey at odds of 133–1, still the highest odds of any Breeders' Cup winner in thirty-four years. Howard and Shannon Nolan's appearance as the only American owners in that winner's circle wouldn't have happened if Howard hadn't decided to check out racing in France many years earlier.

Maybe it was fate. Howard had taken four years of French at Christian Brothers Academy and two years of advanced French at Holy Cross with absolutely no English spoken in class. "I got to be pretty proficient," Howard said. "I was fascinated with the history of France, the glamour of France." Of course, being with Shannon in Paris would only enhance his appreciation of the country.

Howard religiously followed racing by reading the *Daily Racing Form* every day and *The Blood-Horse* magazine every week. "I'd fall asleep at night reading *The Blood-Horse*," Howard said. He was wide awake, however, when he read a story in *The Blood-Horse* about an outbreak in France of contagious equine metritis (CEM), an equine venereal disease that had first appeared on farms in England in 1977.

"There was a ban on exporting and importing horses from France," Howard said. "Shortly after it happened, I was reading an article about an upcoming mixed sale in France in early December in Deauville. I'd been to France, but not to Deauville. I was thinking to myself, they've got this CEM outbreak. There would probably be an opportunity to buy some broodmares cheap and bring them back to Blue Sky Farm. My thinking was that in six months or a year, they would solve the CEM problem and France would open up." Howard got a sales catalog and headed to Deauville.

In France, Howard would make key connections. One of them would ultimately lead him to Arcangues, which is pronounced like King Kong and was named for the village Arcangues in the Pyrenees-Atlantiques department of the Aquitaine region.

Howard had come to know the Murty brothers, Wayne and Duane. "They had a major horse operation, a farm immediately adjacent to Keeneland [the racetrack in Lexington, Kentucky]," Howard said. "They were young guys, very smart, interesting guys. They were new in the business. They brought in stallions, and I made money on every stallion I invested in."

Most of Howard's success came with Top Command, a son of Bold Ruler, the sire of Secretariat. "He was a very good horse in France, just a little below an Arc winner. I think I paid $25,000 for a share, and I bought two shares. I bred to him for four, five years, and in his first crop, along comes Moms Command." That daughter of Top Command won the Filly Triple Crown and was named Champion Three-Year-Old Filly in 1985, multiplying the value of his offspring exponentially. "I sold each share for $135,000, so I was very happy," Howard said.

At Deauville, Wayne Murty's French girlfriend introduced

Howard to Frederick Sauque (pronounced soak), who was the principal bloodstock adviser to Daniel Wildenstein, a celebrated art dealer once called "probably the richest and most powerful art dealer on Earth."

Wildenstein was also a historian and one of the most successful breeder-owners in European racing history. He was a four-time winner of one of Europe's most prestigious races, the Prix de l'Arc de Triomphe, and France's leading owner six times.

Sauque advised Howard on which horses to purchase in the catalog. "He gave me some good advice," Howard said. "I wound up buying several broodmares. The only problem was that I thought the CEM problem would be over in six months to a year. Boy, was I wrong. It lasted three, four years. I had to board my mares in France instead of bringing them to Blue Sky. I left about eight in France. Some were in foal when I bought them. Some were maidens. I bred all of them and sold some of the foals at auction. I was concerned because of the ban, but it turned out okay. I made a little money. When they finally lifted the ban, I brought two broodmares back to the United States."

Plus Value, one of the broodmares Howard brought to Blue Sky, produced Royal Value. Howard called him the fastest horse he ever bred, but also arthritic. "I sold the horse as a yearling to my friend Kevin Langan, who owned seven car dealerships in the Capital District and was a legal client of mine."

Royal Value made his debut in a $50,000 New York–bred stakes for two-year-olds at Finger Lakes on September 27, 1986. The horse nearly didn't make it into the starting gate. "He shipped up from Delaware the day before the race," Howard said. "The trainer, Paul Magnier, was driving the van. Paul is related to John Magnier, who is connected to the Coolmore organization in Ireland. The van broke down on the Pennsylvania Turnpike. They finally got someone to fix the van. He arrived at Finger Lakes at five o'clock in the morning on race day. Paul took him off the van and galloped him a mile and a half because he was a bit arthritic."

Not too arthritic. Royal Value won wire-to-wire by a nose at 13–1. An extremely small percentage of Thoroughbreds begin their careers with a victory in a stakes race. "Kevin was offered $100,000 by D. Wayne Lukas for the horse and he turned it down," Howard said.

Royal Value won his second start in a $100,000 New York–bred stakes at Belmont Park by 3.75 lengths as the 4–5 favorite. "He led every step of the way, and he was eased in the stretch," Howard said. "Lukas offered Kevin $200,000 for the horse. He called me for advice. I told him, 'Sell him.' He said, 'It's my first good horse and I don't need the money.' He turned him down again."

Disdaining a softer $50,000 stakes for New York–breds for his next race, Royal Value took on open company in a $50,000 stakes. He couldn't have found a tougher assignment. He finished third to Java Gold, who would go on to make history by winning both the Whitney Handicap and Travers Stakes at Saratoga as a three-year-old in 1987.

Royal Value finished his career with two victories, two seconds, and two thirds from fifteen starts with earnings of $158,459.

In the late 1980s, Howard got a proposition from his trainer in France, Charlie Millbank, whose father was once secretary to the queen of England. "He privately wanted to buy a colt named Atakad," Howard said. "He said he would stay in for a quarter, and if I took half, he'd find somebody else for the other quarter. The horse looked like he was going to be a good horse."

Howard agreed, and on June 4, 1989, Atakad ran in the Prix du Jockey Club, also known as the French Derby. Howard and Shannon attended the race. "It was exciting," Howard said. "The French Derby is the best three-year-old race in France." Atakad took an early lead, then raced in second most of the way chasing Old Vic, who was ridden by Steve Cauthen and won the race easily. Unfortunately, Atakad tired badly and finished far back.

Millbank was just one accomplished European horseman Howard got to meet in France. "I got lucky," Howard said. "I met a lot of people I never would have known." One of them, Sauque, delivered the highlight of Howard's lifelong passion of racing and breeding Thoroughbreds.

Sauque called Howard in his office one early summer afternoon in 1993 with a bit of news. Wildenstein was syndicating a half interest in three of his horses. Sauque told Howard that all three would be good investments, and Howard bought two shares in Monde Blue, a sprinter who won group stakes in France and was sold a week before he'd start in the 1993 Breeders' Cup Sprint. "We made a lot of money doing that," Howard said. Monde Blue subsequently finished off the board in the 1993 Breeders' Cup Sprint.

Howard also bought two shares in Marignan. "He became a modest sire in France, nothing great. I bred to him a couple times, but then I stopped."

The third horse was five-year-old Arcangues, a chestnut colt by Sagace out of the Irish River mare Albertine, who was trained by Andre Fabre, widely recognized as one of the best conditioners on the entire planet. Howard bought one share of thirty-six offered for a half interest in Arcangues (Wildenstein kept half). Strictly a grass horse, Arcangues had won a Group 1 stakes, the Prix d'Ispahan in France, on May 30.

On July 3 at Sandown Park in England, Arcangues finished sixth in the Group 1 Eclipse Stakes. "He had stumbled coming off the plane in London at Heathrow and fell down before the race," Howard said. "He seemed to be okay when he got up."

Fabre thought so and originally pointed him to the Group 1 Arc, a race in which he'd finished seventh the previous year. "Ten days before the Arc, Fabre told Wildenstein that he wanted to change the game plan and run him the day before in the Group 2 Prix Dollar," Howard said. The reason? The Prix Dollar was a mile and three-sixteenths; the Arc a mile and a half. "Fabre felt that Arcangues didn't really want to run a mile and a half. All week of the Arc, it poured rain in Paris. The course was a bog, soaked with rain for the Prix Dollar. The course was very heavy. The only time he'd run on a heavy course, he ran poorly."

Indeed. Arcangues had finished seventh in a Group 1 stakes on a heavy course earlier that year, and he didn't run well in the Prix Dollar, finishing fourth by ten lengths in the field of five.

Arcangues had been nominated to the $3 million Breeders' Cup Classic at Santa Anita five weeks after the Prix Dollar, but he had never raced on dirt. Unbeknownst to Howard, Fabre decided to work Arcangues on Wildenstein's private dirt track, which was named for his outstanding mare All Along, in Lamorlay, a suburb of Chantilly. Working with a dozen other horses—many trainers in France like to work horses with a lot of company—Arcangues finished first, twenty lengths ahead of the horse in second. Because the workout was on a private track, very few people would know about it.

Soon afterward, Howard received a call. "Sauque was all excited on the phone. He told me, 'We're going to the

141

Breeders' Cup.'" Howard thought Sauque meant the Breeders' Cup Turf. "But Sauque said, 'No, he's going in the Breeders' Cup Classic.' Then he told me about the work, and that Arcangues liked the dirt better than turf. That was a shock. I told Sauque, 'Good—you have to join us for dinner after the Breeders' Cup.' But he said he wasn't coming—just the horse."

Howard called a couple of friends, including Fred Martin, who was a partner on another horse in the Classic, Colonial Affair. That horse had won the 1993 Belmont Stakes under Hall-of-Famer Julie Krone, making her the first woman to win a Triple Crown race. Colonial Affair would finish thirteenth in the Classic.

Howard also called Albany mayor Jerry Jennings. "I told him to bet two dollars across the board on Arcangues. I figured he'd be 20- or 30-1. Nobody would know about the work."

Howard rarely bet more than a hundred dollars on a horse, but he did make exceptions. The best was on May 5, 1984, when Big Bet, who hadn't raced in five and a half months, stepped into the starting gate for the Grade 1 Carter Handicap. "I was an inveterate reader, and there was an article by Joe Hirsch in the *Daily Racing Form*," Howard said. "He quoted trainer Sonny Hines saying, 'The horse was working lights out,' and he felt the horse would have a really good chance to win the Carter off works. I went to the Carter that year. I was studying the *Form*. The horse had been working real well. Bet Big started at 7-1 and went off at 14-1. I liked the horse. I wasn't going to let his odds deter me. I had saved some money I'd won from the winter the year before." Howard bet five hundred to win and five hundred to place on Bet Big. "Biggest bet I ever made," he said. Bet Big won by a half-length. "I made a lot of money," Howard said, laughing.

"The Breeders' Cup World Championships," as Shannon

reflected, "was the brilliant idea of John Gaines of Gaines Dog Food fame. It is Thoroughbred racing's definitive year-end event and honors the best in the sport. It includes two days of world-class racing: usually twelve races, each with prize money (a "purse") of more than $1 million. There is a category to suit the preferences of all Thoroughbreds entered from any participating country. It does not restrict entrants by age, unlike the Triple Crown races, which are only for three-year-olds. It does not dictate that the races be only a certain distance or on a particular surface. There is something for every top-caliber horse, male or female, young or older."

She continued, "The event is supported by nomination fees from breeders around the world when a foal is born. The crown jewel of the two-day event is the Classic, a dirt race run at one and a quarter miles that now has a purse of $6 million. It is for three-year-olds and up, male or female. The horses carry weight based on a handicap system, meaning older horses and those with better records carry more weight. Females get a three-pound weight allowance. On this day, Bertrando, who was a contender for Horse of the Year honors, carried 125 pounds, Best Pal-- the popular California champion-- carried 124 pounds, and Arcangues, although he had won the Prix d'Isphan (FR-1) a few months earlier in France, carried 123 pounds."

Every other year, the event is at a different location in the United States, with the exception of one year when it was in Canada. Howard was one of the original board members. He and Shannon try to go to the event every year.

In 1993, the Breeders' Cup was hosted by the Santa Anita Race Course in Arcadia (near Pasadena) California. The Nolans had seats with one of their daughters, Kathy, and their friends the Martins.

As they were looking for their seats, whom did they see

but some Albanians (from Albany, New York): former Albany mayor Tom Whalen and Key Bank executive Rick Sherman. Although Howard gave them a tip about his horse, they didn't take him seriously after looking at the horse's form.

As the Nolans glanced up to check the odds, they were shocked to see that their foreign import was 99–1 (the highest number that can be shown on the tote board at that time).

"Mike Smith," Shannon recalled, "one of the leading riders in California, was scheduled to ride Arcangues, but when Devil His Due became available via trainer Allen Jenkens, he quickly jumped to the preferred mount."

"Bailey was not having a good day. Even though he had won the Kentucky Derby on Sea Hero six months earlier, he was zero for three this day and did not have a ride in the big race, although he had refused a few. That's how he ended up on Arcangues. It was ride him or watch the race."

"Nevermind; Bailey would make the most of the cards he was dealt. Having a chance to win, or even getting a piece of the pie, would be good enough. The European way is to drop back, relax the horse, and make one run. That would be the strategy he would use. After looking at the *Racing Form*, reality started setting in. The truth of the matter was that this five-year-old French contender had a lot to overcome: (1) He had shipped in from Paris, and that nine-hour time change (and eleven-and-a-half-hour flight) has doomed many a foreign import. No one knows if it's the jet lag or what, but some just don't acclimate; (2) In addition, the horse had never raced outside France or England, or on dirt; (3) All of his sixteen previous turf races had been on an undulating surface, going in a clockwise direction, not like it's done in the United States. That would be like an athlete changing positions in a sport—not so easy. He would be up against the best of the best dirt horses on the planet."

"There were two positives, though. Arcangues would be carrying less weight. He was used to carrying between 130 and 137 pounds. In this race, he would be carrying 123 pounds. That much weight difference at a mile and a quarter can make a big difference."

"Another consideration," according to Shannon, "was that Fabre, a lawyer by trade, is a world-class equine conditioner. He would not send any of his horses so far away unless he thought they could not only compete, but win. With the addition of the best East Coast rider, arguably in the country, things started to get a little more interesting."

Howard quickly put twenty across the board on the horse. The following recollection is how Shannon remembered what happened that day, as retold by the author.

Howard did not have a lot of momentum going into the Classic. He had lost every race that day, and was down six or seven hundred dollars.

He thought about using a credit card to bet four of five hundred dollars. But both he and Shannon were eager to go to the paddock (the walking ring where the horses are saddled) to see their new horse for the first time. Howard quickly put twenty across the board on the horse.

Everyone knew Howard at all the tracks in New York, but it was a different story in California. He hadn't taken the time to secure the necessary paddock credentials; it hadn't occurred to him that it would be an issue. Getting into the paddock would be a challenge, though. He said to the guard, "We have a horse in this race."

She said, "Yeah, everyone does—badge, please."

"No, really..." Howard insisted.

"Look, I don't make the rules," she shot back.

Shannon said, "And what is your name?"

She responded, "Joy." They went back and forth.

Frustrated, Howard started looking around for a familiar face. Soon, he recognized someone, signaled to him and called out his name.

That person was Earl Mack, a friend and prominent horse owner from New York, whose horse Peteski had been scratched. He saw Howard, came over and rescued the Nolans. "They are with me," he said, and voila, the gate was opened. Finally, the Nolans entered the paddock as they heard the familiar words "Riders up" from the paddock dispatcher. Finding Wildenstein and/or Fabre promised to be a futile quest. The place was packed.

Shortly before, Bailey had come out to get on a horse he had never seen, let alone ridden. He too was unable to find Fabre, who speaks perfect English. His two assistants, however, didn't speak a word of English.

Finally, Fabre caught up to Bailey at the end of the tunnel, but the crowd noise was too loud, and it was impossible to hear the trainer's instructions.

Meanwhile, the stage was being set. Lights, please. As if on cue, in the background, the sun was starting to sink behind the majestic purple San Gabriel Mountains as far as the eye could see. The towering, rail-thin palm trees, which seemed to defy gravity, were swaying gently in the breeze scattered throughout the infield ... It was a postcard-picture-perfect day in the country's most popular state weatherwise, with just the slightest hint of chill in the air.

There was a festive atmosphere as a group of smartly dressed international patrons gathered around the vintage 100-foot bar high up in the clubhouse with a spectacular view of the racetrack and the mountains beyond. Conversations were lively among the businesspeople, socialites, celebrities, and die-hard horse fans, all enjoying the moment. Champagne and Chardonnay were flowing freely. The sound of foreign accents could be heard softly above the nostalgic Frank Sinatra music playing in the background.

On the ground level, the huge Clydesdales were trotting by, pulling their familiar Budweiser carriage with their Dalmatian on top wagging his tail. Someone famous bellowed out the national anthem. After two days, the time everyone had been waiting for was about to begin.

The bugles sounded, announcing that the horses were coming onto the racetrack in single file. It was show time, and the post parade was beginning. The jockeys with their colorful silks[3] would be introduced along with their mounts and the horses' owners in front of a crowd that had swelled to more than fifty-five thousand. Some racing enthusiasts watch this part of the procession very closely to look for clues by observing the condition of each animal to decide whether they should bet on him or not. Is he sweaty and washed out (showing nerves, perhaps)? Is his coat dappled and his tail brushed out and healthy looking? Is he carrying additional equipment—leg bandages, blinkers, bar shoes? Is he hard to control or rank? All of these little pieces help the analyst form his choices.

A helicopter was circling around trying to get the best angle for the TV camera crews.

Bailey separated from the lead pony and took off, because the European horses are not used to lead ponies.[4] Arcangues wanted to go! He was full of himself, pulling on the reins, prancing around. He must have sensed that something big

---

[3] Silks are the colorful shirts the jockeys wear that indicate who the owners of the horse are—like a family crest. They are meant to be seen at a distance and are made of loose-fitting silk fabric or form-fitting polyester.
[4] Lead ponies prevent the horses in the race from running away and causing valuable lost TV time while they are rounded up and brought back to the group.

was going to happen. Bailey could feel his energy. This was a good sign.

The horses started loading into the starting gate. Unfortunately, Bailey and Co. were assigned the number twelve post (out of thirteen in the race)—way on the outside.

"And they're off," blasted the track announcer, Tom Durkin. Arcangues broke good, and Bailey took him immediately to the rail to save ground. He settled into an easy tenth place during the first half of the race. Bertrando, the favorite (Bobby Frankel, trainer, and Gary Stevens up) appeared to be trying to steal the race by taking the lead and never looking back. His stable mate, Marquetry, would help to keep the race honest by ensuring a solid, competitive pace.

Back in the seats, Howard was glued to his binoculars, switching from watching Betrando, in front, to fanning to Colonial Affair, and then fanning to Arcangues, back and forth. He would keep doing this. Marquetry (the speed horse) was in the mix as well as Ezzoud and Missionary Ridge. No one was paying any attention to Arcangues, since he was not expected to win or even have a chance. Most serious handicappers had written him off. Too many negatives. Consequently, no pressure for this duo—nice.

Around the final turn, Bailey, still on the inside near the rail, began to ask his horse for more. He started inching closer to the mid-pack as his horse began to hit his best stride. The track announcer, sighting the move, began to raise his voce in anticipaton for what might come, his emotions on display. At the one-sixteenth pole, they passed Ezzoud, the other European entry. Howard noticed Colonial Affair, seventh, was beginning to fade, but when he saw Arcangues suddenly accelerate, his heart started to beat faster. Then suddenly, there was light. A little space opened up between Kissin Kris and Marquetry ...

Arcangues shot through the hole like a bullet. The announcer could be heard saying, "And here comes Arcangues between horses. A huge upset is looming here; he is flying on the outside." Howard, Shannon, Kathy, and the Martins— then it seemed like everyone—were all on their feet screaming, "Go, go, go!"

Now, with only one horse in front of them to beat, it was time to get excited. Yes, they could really win this thing! Then it felt like slow motion. A big red blur passed by Bertrando. The crowd went completely silent as Tom Durkin called out the name of the closer who proved the logic wrong in the final furlong[5]. You could almost hear the collective gasp from everyone watching. "Arcangues," Durkin was now screaming, "and Jerry Bailey have just won the 1993 Breeders' Cup Classic by two lengths"—the volume of his voice rising to a roar—"at 99 to 1!" (It would end up as 133–1, actually, since the tote board goes only to 100.) "This is an impossible victory, pari-mutuelly speaking, an ABSOLUTE SHOCKER!"

Back in the NBC broadcast booth with John Veitch and Tom Hammond, Tom exclaimed, "Are you kidding me? The Europeans finally broke through [after ten years] with an American jockey with the longest priced winner in Breeders' Cup history!"

A stunned Gary Stevens, who thought he had won the race, had the look of disbelief. He had never seen them coming. Ironically—fast-forward a few years—Stevens would make his acting debut in a film about another long shot. It would be called *Seabiscuit*.

Howard won $3,500 on a $60.00 bet ($20.00 across the board). He didn't even mind giving the IRS the 20 percent

---

[5] A furlong equals one-eighth of a mile.

off the top required on any win over $600.00. A $2.00 bet had paid a whopping $269.20. The handle[6] was $82,608,570.

Bailey's career was on a roll after that improbable feat, and within two years (1995) he would be inducted into the Racing Hall of Fame.

Arcangues, the beautiful five-year-old French chestnut[7] colt with the funny name, had just won the most prestigious race on Earth at odds of 133–1. The son of Sagace, 1984 winner of the Prix de l'Arc de Triomphe at Longchamp in Paris, had just made his father proud. Arcangues's race record ended up with six wins, two seconds, and two thirds with winnings of $1,974,631. (The Breeders' Cup awards 55% of the purse to the winner of each of it's races).

Back in Paris, friends said later, it was 3:00 am. Footage of the race was shown on TVG, the French sports TV channel. The crowd in the little Australian sports bar called Moose, on the Left Bank, went wild. "*C'est incroyable!*" they shouted. (It's incredible.) "Vive la France!" (Long live France—way to go; one of our own just won.)

The Wildensteins would bottle a French Bordeaux in honor of the occasion with a picture of Arcangues and Bailey on the label and call it Cuvee Arcangues from the Chateau Coquillas Vinyard (1991). It would be a Grand Vin De Graves, Appelation Pessac Leognan Controlle.

As the Nolans were walking into the trophy presentation enclosure, Shannon caught a glimpse of the paddock security guard who had given them a hard time earlier. As she made eye contact with the guard, Shannon smiled and waved. "Hi, Joy," she said. That felt good.

Terry Liebel of NBC asked Fabre if he had expected the win. "I was confident a month from the race," Fabre said, "...

---

[6] The *handle* is the worldwide amount of money bet on a horse.
[7] A chestnut horse has reddish hair.

[but] as it got closer, I had doubts. He was a good horse in France …[but] he has his days. I knew he would handle the surface; he loves this course." Allen E. Murray, CEO of Mobil Oil Corp., presented the trophy."

Centennial Farms and the Martins, who had included their friends the Nolans, had planned a post-win party for Colonial Affair. The celebration, however, quickly focused on Arcangues's exciting win, which was very gracious of the hosts.

"In the winner's circle, we were with Daniel Wildenstein, his wife, his son Alec, Bailey, and Fabre," Howard said, "And there was Skip Dickstein, from Albany, New York, taking our picture. We were the only Americans who owned any interest in the horse. The thrill of a lifetime. It doesn't get any better than standing in the winner's circle after the Breeders' Cup Classic. Not too many people can say that."

After the Breeders' Cup, a deal to sell Arcangues to Japanese interests fell apart. Wildenstein decided to send Arcangues back to California and aim at the 1994 Santa Anita Handicap with a Hall of Fame trainer, Dick Mandella. An injury prevented Arcangues from making the Big Cap, but he did win the Grade 2 John Henry Handicap by a half-length on grass.

Sticking to turf, Arcangues tired to fifth in the Grade 1 Hollywood Turf Handicap. In what would be his final career start, Arcangues returned to dirt, was reunited with Bailey, and finished fifth in the Grade 1 Hollywood Gold Cup Handicap. Arcangues then fractured a sesamoid and was sold to Kazuo Nakamura, who would stand him at stud in Japan, for much less than in the original deal. But he had taken Howard to the top of the mountain.

Another French colt named Deja didn't quite work out as well.

One of the horsemen Howard had met in France was Alec Head, a prominent French trainer, breeder, and owner of Thoroughbreds who operates his stud farm, the Haras du Quesnay, near Deauville. Howard also met his three children: Martine, who manages the stud farm; Criquette, one of France's leading trainers; and Freddy, a leading jockey and trainer. "I became friendly with Martine, who had a lot of connections in Kentucky," Howard said. "She owned a couple of shares in Bering, who became a top racehorse and stallion in Kentucky for two years and then in France. We did a foal sharing."

Howard had purchased a mare, Doha, one late night in a sale at Keeneland for $4,000. Bering was standing his initial season in Kentucky, and Howard bred Doha to Bering. Doha got in foal, and Howard brought her to Blue Sky Farm. Doha produced a colt, Deja, who was a New York–bred, thus eligible for the nation's richest breeding program for breeders and owners. "He was a big, beautiful colt," Howard said. The name Deja means "already" in French.

In 1990, a foal could also be declared a French-bred if the foal was in France before December 1, an added inducement when Howard offered him for sale in Deauville. "We had the horse in the sale at Deauville in August. That's the big sale," Howard said. "The night before the sale, the horse acted up in the stall, and we had to scratch him from the sale. We had to either sell him or race him. Martine wanted to race him, so I said, 'Let's go.'" Criquette Head would train the colt.

Deja bucked shins,[8] as a two-year-old, and would have minor physical problems throughout his racing career. Howard and Martine gelded him (had his testicles removed due to

---

[8] To *buck shins* is to incur an injury (painful soreness to the front of the horse's legs) usually caused by two or three year olds traveling at high speeds (over 33mph) during the first ten weeks of training

extreme aggresive and hard to handle behavior) and decided to race him in France. Martine's father, Alec, had suggested the procedure. Deja won his first start at Saint-Cloud, but he came out of the race injured. In his second start, he finished out of the money. "Everybody was disappointed," Howard said.

Then Deja won a listed stakes by two lengths as the 4–5 favorite and finished fourth by a length in a Group 2 stakes. "We decided to sell him privately," Howard said. "Martine wanted $500,000. There was an offer of $400,000. I said, 'Take it.' She didn't want to sell. So I got on the next plane to France, and I talked to her father. He tells her to sell him, but she won't budge."

So at the end of 1992, Deja was shipped to resume his racing career in the United States. He wound up in Christophe Clement's barn. His one victory came in the first of six steeplechase races in a maiden[9] $5,000 claimer. "We wound up selling him in a paddock sale at Belmont for $5,000," Howard said.

He's still trying to figure out why Martine didn't take the $400,000.

---

[9] a maiden race is offered for horses that have never won a race.

Chapter 15

A YEAR OF CHANGE

In 1994, Howard announced his retirement from the New York State Senate, flirted with becoming Albany County Democratic chairman, pulled his name from consideration for that position, and prepared for a new chapter in his life.

"I had decided not to run for a senate seat again," Howard said. "I was getting burned out, going out night after night to all these functions. I was getting older—not old, but older. Lee Aronowitz, who had retired from politics and moved to Puerto Rico, had been my campaign manager. I wasn't spending much time at the law practice, even though I was one of the three senior partners. So I just decided I wanted to go out and practice law."

Actually, Howard had considered retirement two years earlier, but some of his friends who were leaders in the Democratic Party had persuaded him to run again. Howard had done so, winning reelection easily.

Howard announced on February 14 that he would not be seeking an eleventh term in the New York State Senate. A week later, an editorial in the *Times Union*, although mentioning his absenteeism and personal business interests, also saluted his positive effect:

The issue—He says it is time to move on despite his growing political influence. Our opinion—His leadership on social issues and party reform won't be easy to replace …

No one could quarrel with Senator Nolan's legislative priorities—and not only on state issues. It was the senator who warned Albany County Democratic bosses that times were changing, and the machine had to change as well. Long before the term limit movement gained momentum, it was Senator Nolan who urged those same bosses to groom younger candidates who could lead the party into the future.

More than most politicians, Senator Nolan could see the future when those around him were consumed by the press of the moment. That's the mark of leadership.

In a letter to the editor published by the *Times Union* on April 22, Larry King, who was Howard's close adviser for several years, offered a personal thank-you: "Senator Nolan has served the residents of Albany County with dignity and pride the past 20 years. Senator Nolan has been a champion for each and every one of his constituents, regardless of political affiliation. Thank you, Senator Nolan, for your guidance and dedicated service. You have been an inspiration to us all. Your achievements and compassion will not be forgotten."

Howard didn't go out quietly in his final year in the senate. In his June "Legislative report from Senator Howard C. Nolan," which was sent to all of his constituency, he blamed the governor and legislative leaders for failing to pass a state budget on time, by April 1, for the tenth consecutive year: "The shamefully overdue state budget poses particular hardships for our schools, for Albany County government, and for local groups awaiting funds that will allow them to continue operating on our behalf."

Howard proposed that "no appropriation bills be passed. No emergency spending bills that make it too easy to let the process drag on and on without any resolution. Not now, and never after March 31 if a budget cannot be implemented by its legal deadline."

On June 20, Howard endorsed highly respected Jim McCaffrey, a former Albany County Social Services commissioner who worked for Catholic Charities, to run for Howard's seat in the senate against Mike Hoblock, the Republican Albany County executive. "Jim is a man of great personal character and has done a great job in the past," Howard told Mike McKeon of the *Times Union*. Hoblock, though, would win the election.

But leaving politics would be harder than Howard had imagined. In mid-September, he emerged as a leading contender to replace Cohoes Mayor Robert Signoracci as Albany Country Democratic chairman. Until then, seventy-one-year-old Appellate Division Justice Leonard Weiss had been mentioned as Signoracci's likely successor.

"I was not thinking of running for chairman," Howard said, "but I had backed Jerry Jennings for mayor, and he won. I busted my ass for him." Howard continued with the story:

> Then Signoracci decided not to run, so Jerry wanted me to run. He set up a meeting with Leonard Weiss, me, and him. Leonard was a friend of mine. The first thing Jerry said to Leonard was, "Leonard, I know you want to be chairman, but I'm going to support Howard Nolan."
>
> Leonard told Jerry, "I'd like to be chairman, but if you support Howard, I'll support him."
>
> Then Joe McElroy, a ward leader and a big supporter of Jerry's, said he would like to be the

chairman. When Jerry told Joe he was going to
support me, Joe said, "I'm running anyway."
And he had some political allies.

I would have won easily. I'd worked with people in the party for years and most of them
liked me. But the more I thought about it, I
decided that was a fight I didn't want to be in. I
wasn't going to spur a big fight for the position,
which would have split the Democratic party.

So less than a week after the public had learned that
Howard wanted to be chairman, he suddenly withdrew his
name from consideration. "After doing a lot of soul search-
ing, I came to the conclusion that I could win the battle but
the Democratic Party was going to lose the war," Howard
told Mike McKeon in the *Times Union*. McKeon wrote that
Howard had "sparked sharp opposition in some quarters
when he announced a bid for the post last week."

In Howard's place, Weiss was elected chairman. In doing so, he gave up four years on the bench with an annual
salary of $114,817 to become chairman and go into private
law practice. In a statement that Howard issued, announcing he would not run for chairman, he had endorsed Weiss,
saying, "Leonard Weiss is a distinguished judge and a fine
gentleman. He has the respect and admiration of all who
know him."

A *Times Union* editorial addressed Howard's decision to
back out:

There never was any question that State Senator
Howard Nolan possessed the qualifications to
be the next party chairman. Indeed, the senator had seemed to be the odds-on favorite. He

has the seasoning of years in political office as well as in the engine room of party headquarters. He's helped take the Democrats out of the machine era and into today's political arena, where new ideas—and honest dissent—have replaced fear and silence. Perhaps, more than any other Democrat, Senator Nolan has seen how crucial it is for the party to nurture tomorrow's candidates, instead of clinging tenaciously to the old ways. Even so, the senator's profile as a reformer has earned him deep resentment from members of the Old Guard.

In mid-November, a letter from Patrick Bulgaro, the president and executive director of the Center for the Disabled, wrote a thank-you letter to the editor that appeared in every Capital District newspaper. The letter cited Howard's decades of service, his role as a member of the board of directors since 1963, his chairmanship of the Foundation Board, the fact that a residence center in Loudonville housing seven children with disabilities is named Nolan House, and that Howard had won the organization's Humanitarian of the Year Award in 1984.

Howard had been the president and chairman of the board when the Center for the Disabled's new building was constructed on Manning Boulevard, across the street from St. Peter's Hospital, where Howard had served on the board for twelve years.

"Howard Nolan's legacy, though, goes beyond these contributions of time, dollars, and talent," Bulgaro wrote. "He is quite simply a friend to all of us. When he visits our school programs, our students call him by his first name. He stops to observe the latest communication technology in action. He believes in the work we do with individuals who have disabilities and their families, and through him many members of the community have become involved in the center. Thousands of individuals with disabilities have had richer and fuller lives because of his work."

In December 1994, Howard said goodbye to his constituency in his final "Legislative report from Senator Howard C. Nolan":

> Dear Friend, I write this last newsletter with a great deal of mixed emotions. On the one hand, it has given me enormous enjoyment and pleasure to have the good fortune to serve the citizens of the 42nd Senate District for 20 years. It's really been a tremendous experience to touch the lives of so many people over this period of time. For this reason, it is sad to say goodbye to my life as state Senator and to all of you whom I've had the privilege of representing.
>
> On the other hand, as you may imagine, my work in the New York State Senate, coupled with my other professional responsibilities, has left me little time to spend with my family. It is appropriate to now move on with my life and to enjoy more time with my wife, Shannon, my children, and my grandchildren.

That was on the front page of the final newsletter. The other three pages were all photos of Howard over the previous twenty years and a staff picture of Dwayne Williams, Barbara Jensen, Barbara Zwack, Nebraska Brace, Christina Gifford, Michael Flynn, Nona Teabout, Charles Gaddy, and Patrick McCarville.

On December 13, at the Omni Hotel in downtown Albany,

a retirement gala for Howard was held. Music was provided by the Albany Symphony Orchestra. About six hundred people, including politicians from both parties, attended the event. "My daughter Debbie, representing my family, made a big speech," Howard said. "That's what I remember—she made a very passionate speech about my service. I was proud of her, and I still am. She runs both shopping plazas."

Two and a half months later, Howard was honored at the Catholic Conference's annual Public Policy Forum. On behalf of Cardinal John O'Connor, the archbishop of New York, Bishop Howard Hubbard presented Howard the New York State Catholic Conference Public Policy Award for his "courageous public service in the state senate from 1975 to 1994 representing the Forty-Second Senatorial District."

Both Joyce Roman and Barbara Zwack, who worked for Howard for years, saw his service every single day. "I can tell you this—he was always upbeat," said Roman, who was Howard's administrative assistant in the senate, then the office manager at Heller and Nolan. "I never saw him unpleasant or out of sorts. He had very strong moral convictions. He was tireless. He had a mind like a steel trap. He expected a lot from his employees, but he set the pace. If you weren't willing to work hard, then it didn't work out."

Zwack, who worked for Howard with HMC Associates and in the senate, where she still works today, said of her boss, "I never saw him tired. I just can't believe how he can juggle. He had so many things going on: the senate, horses, the plazas, the law office. It amazed me how he handled all those things. I don't know how he did it. It was amazing."

Chapter 16

PRISONERS AND HORSES

"Some people see things the way they are and say why. I dream things that never were and say why not?" This George Bernard Shaw quotation was cited by both John F. Kennedy and Robert F. Kennedy.

In 1980, Monique Koehler, a casual racing fan in Long Island, read an Ed Comerford article in *Newsday* about Daphne Collins, a trainer who was trying to find homes for Thoroughbreds after their racing days were over to ensure they did not wind up being sold for slaughter.

"My brother had taken me to Belmont Park, and I had never seen anything so beautiful in my life," said Koehler, who now lives in Wheat Ridge, just outside Denver, Colorado. "I'd never been physically close to a horse. I didn't ride." Koehler says that after she wrote to Collins with a donation, "She called me up and said she had to meet me. So I met her for dinner in a restaurant in Jericho."

At that dinner, Collins implored her to take over the program. Koehler agreed to do so, but then she made a frightening discovery. "I realized there was nothing for these horses," she said. "These horses leaving the racetrack had nowhere to go, or they were going to slaughter. I became fixated and told myself, 'I am going to get this thing done.'"

In 1983, Koehler founded the Thoroughbred Retirement Foundation (TRF), and Howard was on the original TRF board. When Koehler mentioned to him her goal of finding homes for retired Thoroughbreds, Howard had an idea:

> I had Blue Sky Farm, which was right near the Wallkill prison, a couple of miles away as the crow flies. Every time I went back and forth to the farm from Albany, I'd go by the Wallkill prison. They had a farm there that they weren't using. A light went on and I thought to myself, *Wouldn't this be great, if we could join with the state and find something to do for the prisoners?* They had the land and the built-in labor, the prisoners, who would learn about horse racing and how to care for the horses and gain a skill that would be marketable when they got out. So it was a natural. It was a way to use the land, to develop the skills of prisoners, and, from the horsemen's point of view, to have a farm for retired horses. That's how it happened. It was a win-win situation, a win for the prison system and a win for the retired racehorse with no place to go. A lot of them were being sent to slaughterhouses.

(Horse slaughter in the United States ended in 2007, but American horses are still being exported to Canada and Mexico for slaughter.)

First, however, the TRF board had to endorse the program. "When Howard showed up at the board meeting and said, 'Here's my idea,' several board members refused to support it," said Diana Pikulski, the TRF's director of external affairs.

Pikulski had joined TRF after she gave a riding lesson to Koehler—the first and last of her life—and her son at a stable in Middletown, New Jersey, where Koehler had relocated. When Koehler fell and broke her arm after just starting TRF, she called Pikulski and offered her a job as her driver for the summer before Pikulski started college. Pikulski agreed and is still working for the TRF and helping horses.

Koehler loved Howard's idea: "It was tremendous. It was in response to me whining about not being able to find a place for these horses. It was brilliant, absolutely brilliant."

A couple of board members resigned over the issue, but other board members were delighted with the idea and endorsed it. The TRF then received approval from the New York State Department of Corrections. The program was a go. The TRF would appropriately call it Second Chances.

Koehler visited the farm. "It's such an amazing place," she said. "It was a dilapidated dairy farm. I went up there and I loved it. We had a facility to show people that horses could be saved, that horses could still contribute to man in the most meaningful way possible. I wasn't going to let anything get in the way of it."

Koehler reached out to several industry leaders, including Penny Chenery, owner of two-time Horse of the Year and Triple Crown winner Secretariat; Martha Gerry, owner of three-time Horse of the Year Forego; Allaire Du Pont, owner of five-time Horse of the Year Kelso; trainers Skippy Shapoff and Peter Howe; and sportswriter Elinor Penna, the widow of trainer Angel Penna Sr. All offered their support. Then Gerry and Du Pont allowed their famous horses to return to Belmont Park on October 26, 1983, in a special appearance to raise funds for Second Chances.

The TRF hired Jim Tremper, a former Standardbred farm manager from nearby Pine Bush. Initially hired as project manager, Tremper was later named the vocational instructor for the Department of Corrections. He's still there in 2017 and is rightfully proud of the four hundred Thoroughbreds and five hundred prisoners who have participated in Wallkill's Second Chances. The program is so successful that it's being done by the TRF in Massachusetts, Maryland, Virginia, South Carolina, Florida, Illinois, Indiana, and Kentucky.

"There was nothing like this ever," Pikulski said, and she salutes Howard for getting Second Chances started. "The thing about him is just how pure his love of horses is, and also his concerns for all people. Obviously, he's a guy who has served the public and he's just never about himself. Howard got it right. He said, 'This is going to work.' It's his can-do attitude. That's how you change problems in society. Those prisoners deserve a second chance, like everybody does. Like every horse does."

Promised Road was the first Thoroughbred to enter Second Chances, on July 26, 1984.

What's most amazing about this program is the relationship between horse and prisoner. Asked what percentage of inmates are scared when they make first contact with the horse, Tremper said "Ninety-eight percent. Very few of them have no fear when they start. That's really rare."

What happens next is up to the prisoner. "It totally changes the way these guys do business," Tremper said. "They're used to taking things, whatever they want and whenever they want. The horse won't allow it. If you brought a bad attitude to the farm, you can't do anything with the horse. You have to make the horse want to cooperate. I've seen it so many times. If they come with any negative attitude, they have to change to get anything done. Horses read people so well."

Koehler is particularly proud of one inmate who made it through the program and became a counselor with the New York State Department of Corrections. "He was a smart young guy who got involved with drugs, was on the streets, got in trouble, and was in prison," Kohler said. "He credited the program with saving his life. He went to another prison and is doing consultation work for prisoners and drug users. I am very proud because he's my friend."

Of course, the horses benefit from the program, too. "These horses that are infirmed and crippled? Making them right so they can enjoy the rest of their lives is great," Tremper said.

Tremper said the Second Chances recidivism rate is much lower than other vocational prison programs in New York State. "The biggest change we see here is that the prisoners don't get in trouble when they stay in the program." According to Tremper, prisoners have stayed with the program for as little as one week and as long as twelve years. "The program is an amazing thing," he added.

Howard was invited to speak at Second Chances' thirty-year anniversary party in 2014. "I talked about the genesis of how it started and what a success it has been," he said. "I was proud to be the person who initiated it. New York was the first state to do it, and I'm proud of that, too."

Chapter 17

MOVING ON

Howard's retirement from public office didn't end his influence and contributions to the Albany County Democratic Party and the New York State Senate. Republican Michael Hoblock, a former three-time New York State assemblyman, had already scored a gigantic upset when he was elected Albany County executive in November 1991. In the election for Howard's district in 1994, he did it again, defeating Jim McCaffrey, whom Howard had backed.

In 1996, Howard supported attorney Neil Breslin, who had never run for public office, to defeat Hoblock in his bid for reelection. "Howard's the one, when the Democrats lost the seat, who said, 'We'll pick up the seat if we don't get a political hack,'" Breslin said. "Howard was the one who pushed me to run for the senate, the single person. Howard was very supportive."

Breslin won the senate election and two reelections for the Forty-Second District, then five more two-year terms for the redrawn Forty-Sixth District and two more for the redrawn Forty-Fourth District. In total, he served ten terms in the senate. Combined with Howard's previous dominance, the Democrats controlled a senate seat for forty of forty-two years.

Leaving the senate had given Howard more time. Then he stopped practicing law in 1997. "I decided to stop for several reasons," Howard said. "My dad, who was my best friend later in life, died from a heart attack when he was sixty-four. He never got to enjoy the fruits of retirement. He was going to retire after turning sixty-five. He and my mother were going to travel a lot, but he never got to live that. He had survived a bad heart attack the previous September. With modern medicine, he probably would have lived into his eighties. I could afford to stop practicing law, and I had a great wife. I've still got my license. I had two things to keep me busy: real estate and horses."

With horses, he took on two major roles. In 1997, the New York Racing Association, a quasi, not-for-profit entity that runs Aqueduct, Belmont Park, and Saratoga Race Course, was fighting for its legal life. Its franchise would expire at the end of 1997, and its reputation had been tarnished by a multitude of scandals through the early to midnineties. So bidders from around the world were lining up to replace the NYRA.

Headed by Howard, the mysterious Center to Preserve Racing was a think tank of prominent Thoroughbred owners and breeders. They called for NYRA to be replaced by a for-profit company, without endorsing any single group bidding for the franchise, which led to speculation that they were interested in getting the franchise. Howard denied that, but the only statement the Center to Preserve Racing made was "Thoroughbred racing must be given an opportunity to compete in a national and international marketplace by focusing on market-driven forces rather than political expediency."

However, in the late-night hours of a late August evening, the New York legislature and Governor George Pataki extended NYRA's franchise another ten years, through 2007. That decision was so controversial that the legislature and Pataki made it known with a press release on the late Saturday afternoon of Saratoga's biggest race, the Grade 1 Travers Stakes, the Mid-Summer Derby. The timing guaranteed that the press release would generate much less attention in the media because of the Travers.

In 1998, Howard was elected to the first of two terms as president of the New York Thoroughbred Breeders. He would not run for a third term. "I've enjoyed it, but I don't plan on another term," he told Karen Johnson, an accomplished journalist whose beloved dad, Phil, was a Hall of Fame trainer. In a November 2, 2001, story in the *Daily Racing Form*, Howard told Johnson that his greatest satisfaction came from getting the three separate entities of New York racing—NYRA, the New York Thoroughbred Horsemen's Association, and the New York Thoroughbred Breeders—to work together. "I think we really have made great strides in the New York breeding program by bringing the industry together," he said. "That cooperation has put us on the same page as a group. That may have been lacking in the past."

Howard told Johnson that the NYTB had been operating in the black for four years, as the New York Thoroughbred Breeding Development Fund's incentive program reached $9 million in breeder, owner, and stallion awards. Soon Howard, himself, would be earning those awards as a co-owner of the best home-bred he ever raced.

Howard's lifelong friend Fred Martin took a different path to Thoroughbred horsemanship than Howard. "We took very different routes into the racing industry," Martin said. "Howard was very interested in hitting a home run by buying stock at very reasonable prices at the sales. I didn't see that as a route I wanted to go. I was hoping to get a very good horse. I tried the only route I could take: buy a small percentage in a partnership. We kind of developed our own business in parallel directions."

Martin's partnership with Centennial Farms gave him the thrill of a lifetime. Colonial Affair made Triple Crown history by winning the 1993 Belmont Stakes, the final leg of the Triple Crown, under Hall of Famer Julie Krone. Then Colonial Affair added another Grade 1 stakes, the Whitney Handicap at Saratoga, with Hall of Fame jockey Jose Santos in the saddle.

"When the horse retired, I kept my interest in him and had two shares to breed," Martin said. "Colonial Affair was not nearly as good in the breeding shed as he was on the race-track. His stud fee kept going down. When it got to $3,500, I said, 'I've always wondered about taking a shot. It's time to be a breeder.'"

Martin called Howard and asked him if he wanted to be a partner. Howard agreed, and they bred Howard's mare, A Rose for Shannon—named for Shannon—to Colonial Affair. A Rose for Shannon produced Irish Colonial, who turned out to be a top turf horse from 2001 to 2006. Martin and Howard hired Hall of Famer Scotty Schulhofer, who had been train-ing for Centennial, to train Irish Colonial. "Scotty came up to my farm to see the horse, and he loved the horse," Howard said. Then Scotty retired just three races into Irish Colonial's career, and Scotty's son, Randy, took over as trainer.

Irish Colonial won two stakes for New York–breds, the 2003 Kingston and the 2004 Mohawk, and came close several times to winning a graded stakes in open company, finish-ing third by a half-length in both the Grade 3 Lexington at Belmont Park and the Grade 3 Saranac at Saratoga in 2003. In 2004, Irish Colonial finished third by three-quarters of a length in the Grade 2 Bernard Baruch Handicap at Saratoga.

Irish Colonial retired with six victories, two seconds, and seven thirds from twenty-nine starts with earnings of $397,068. Better yet for Howard and Martin, he also earned New York–bred bonus money of close to $80,000.

Later, Howard bred Readtheprospectus, a son of Read the Footnotes out of Howard's mare Near Bethany, a daughter of Affirmed, a Triple Crown champion and two-time Horse of the Year. Howard sold him for $30,000 as a two-year-old in training in Ocala, Florida, in 2012. Then he watched the horse turn into an outstanding gelding who won two New York–bred stakes under the care of trainer Chad Brown, who, like Howard, is a native of Mechanicville.

Readtheprospectus made his first two starts on dirt, finishing second and third at Saratoga. Brown switched him to the turf, and he finished fourth in a maiden race at Belmont. Then he forgot how to lose. Readtheprospectus won a maiden grass race at Belmont by four lengths and then his first six starts as a four-year-old. Many horses don't win seven races in their entire career—Readtheprospectus won seven straight.

The horse eventually had physical problems, got claimed four times, and finished his career with ten wins, two seconds, and two thirds from twenty starts with earnings topping a half-million dollars. As the breeder of Readtheprospectus, Howard wound up getting more than $100,000 in New York–bred bonus awards. "It's the best breeding program in the country," Howard said, and he had helped get it there.

Chapter 18

ARGENTINA BECKONS

Howard was sitting in his box seat at Gulfstream Park in early 2002 when Duane Murty stopped by to say hello. Murty had been impressed by Forty Marinesca, a filly up for sale in Argentina, and he asked Howard if he might be interested in buying her. "I read every periodical I could about horse racing," Howard said, "and I had noticed over the years that Argentina had sent many horses to the United States who had performed well, including Forli, who became a very good sire in the United States."

Forty Marinesca was doing well in Argentina. She had finished second in a field of nine in a Group 2 stakes and third by three-quarters of a length in a field of eleven in a Group 1 stakes, February 23, 2002, before Howard went down to Argentina.

Howard told Murty he was interested and made plans to visit Buenos Aires with Shannon and inspect the filly. "I had never been there before," Howard said. "It intrigued me because Argentina was one of the richest countries in South America. Shannon had been to Buenos Aires a few times. So we arranged to meet Duane Murty to look at the filly. Physically, she looked very good. I wound up buying her for around $75,000 despite knowing that she had a minor throat problem." Howard shipped her to the United States, where she won a couple of races and placed in three stakes. "She was okay," Howard said. "She made about $100,000."

Shannon said, "Howard has a natural ability to take risks that are good investments." Of course, that didn't preclude occasional bad investments.

Howard and Shannon, neither of whom spoke Spanish, had decided they'd stay in Buenos Aires for a week whether or not they purchased the filly. Murty hooked Howard and Shannon up with the daughter of the racing secretary at Palermo, Argentina's largest racetrack, and she helped the Nolans find a good hotel. It would be Hotel Cristoforo Colombo.

"It was a beautiful place in a nice section of Buenos Aires (Palermo)," Howard said. "We paid the equivalent of fifty dollars a night. In New York it would have cost three hundred a night. We went out every night. You could buy the best steaks in the world for ten dollars and a bottle of wine in a very good restaurant for nine or ten dollars. They're known for their red wine, Malbec, which is equivalent to a good Bordeaux in France. What struck me was the worst slums you could ever imagine outside Buenos Aires. The contrast between the slums and the main area of Buenos Aires was like night and day. In Buenos Aires, there were a lot of places for sale."

When they returned to the United States, Howard and Shannon decided they would return to Buenos Aires and look at apartments. "The prices were really cheap," Howard said. Shannon added, "The city has old-world charm, and it's beautifully designed and landscaped with many parks and stunning architecture." Howard found a real estate agent in

Buenos Aires through his friend Jim O'Connell, a real estate agent in Fort Lauderdale.

Howard and Shannon returned to Buenos Aires three months after their first visit and hooked up with the real estate agent there. They looked at two apartments and settled on one in Recoleta, near the United States and British Embassies. Howard described it as one of the nicest neighborhoods in the city, with many hotels, restaurants, and shops. "Three bedrooms, three bathrooms, and a maid's quarters or a fourth bedroom," Howard said. "We wound up buying it. For the next six years, we went down there five or six times a year for one or two weeks at a time. I had retired from the law practice so I had time, lots of time."

When they bought the apartment, the Nolans also purchased another horse. India Halo won a Group 3 stakes before finishing third in a Group 1 and second in a Group 2, and then racing in the United States with trainer Michael Matz. Howard bought her for $150,000 in cash. Eventually, she'd also race for trainers Jim Ferraro in New York and Tim Ritvo in Florida. She won three ungraded stakes in the United States and finished her career with six victories, six seconds, and four thirds from thirty-three starts with earnings of $283,308.

Howard kept India Halo as a broodmare. In a foal-sharing agreement with Frank Stronach, the owner of Gulfstream Park, Santa Anita, and other racetracks, India Halo was bred to Ghostzapper, producing a small colt who sold for $20,000 as a yearling at the Keeneland September Sale. He was bought by a Swedish trainer and was named AGhostInGodsPlace. He raced in Sweden and France with above average success. Another foal-sharing with Stronach sent India Halo to Awesome Again. She produced a small filly who wound up making $39,000 despite bone chips. Then she was bred to

Giralomo twice; Howard still has one of those two foals and may race her.

Howard and Shannon also became friends with Antonio Bullrich an auctioneer and the president of the racing association that ran Palermo, and his wife. "He was also a major breeder and owner in Argentina," Howard said. "We were introduced by Nestor, the racing secretary at Palermo. We used to keep some horses at his farm about two and half hours from Buenos Aires. We stayed overnight at their ranch. Had dinner with them or lunch many times. Just really very, very friendly people."

In 2009, though, Shannon and Howard decided to sell their apartment in Buenos Aires. "The political situation was becoming unstable, and many American companies were leaving," Shannon said.

They had paid $175,000 for the apartment, and reached an agreement to sell it for $260,000. "At the time—it's changed since—all real estate transactions in Argentina, especially closings, were paid for in dollars, not pesos," Howard said. He had to hire a money changer to handle the transaction, which occurred in a private building.

The buyer, an international import agent, put several backpacks on the table. "He started pulling out packs of one-hundred dollar bills and put them on the table," Shannon said. "I told him, 'You've got to be kidding.'" He wasn't. The pile of cash was about five feet wide by two feet deep and about eighteen inches high, according to Shannon.

"They had a money guy counting the money, and I had a guy counting the money," Howard said. "They wired the money to me in an account in New York a week later. We haven't been back since."

Chapter 19

ALL IN THE FAMILY

Family remains a vital component of Howard's life. His seven children, born in a span of just eight and a half years, had to navigate through Howard's long separation and divorce from his first wife, Gerrie; a frightening medical hardship that Howard's daughter Kathy conquered; and the tragic loss of Howard's seventeen-year-old granddaughter Christine, who was killed in a horse riding accident.

But the second generation of Nolans have achieved success by relying on many of the qualities that Howard and Gerrie instilled in them. They've welcomed Howard's second wife, Shannon, and produced eleven beloved grandchildren.

Of Howard's seven children, only his middle child, Bob, is a son. "It was interesting to say the least," Bob said. "Six sisters, a mother, and a father on the road. It was me against the world." He laughed and continued, "I became good friends with my sisters."

Now fifty-four, Bob is a retired risk management director for Citibank in New York City. He says that when he was younger, he didn't get to see his dad a lot. "Especially in the days of the senate, he was always on the run. He's a very driven person. It's interesting and inspiring to watch his energy and passion. He was doing it for the right reasons, because he always wanted to help people."

When Bob was a teenager, Howard was trying to figure out how to help his rebellious son. "I was rebellious, not unlike a lot of young boys," Bob said. "I knew everything in the world, and my parents didn't know anything. I was anti-establishment." His dad, of course, was the establishment, but that was just part of the problem.

"Bob and I had kind of a tumultuous relationship during those years, because I wound up leaving his mother," Howard said. "He was a little bit wild, and I wasn't happy with how he was performing academically. He wasn't living up to his bright smarts."

Howard went to Christian Brothers Academy to meet with Vice Principal Ned McGraw, who had been Howard's high school teammate in basketball and baseball. Ned told Howard, "You don't need to worry about Bob," and then he explained why. Two months earlier, Ned had received a call from an elderly woman. Driving on Route 787 on a snowy day, she had lost control of her car and gotten stuck in a snowbank. A couple of minutes later, a car had pulled up. A boy wearing a CBA uniform got out and fixed the problem. She had tried to give him money, but he wouldn't take it. After that phone call, as Ned told Howard, he knew that Bob was turning out just fine.

Bob remembers the incident: "It was a snowy day. I was dropping my sister Karen off at Saint Pius, and some woman had just run into a snowbank. I saw her getting out of her car, so I stopped and asked if everything was okay. She had a piece of metal sticking into a tire. I was able to pull the metal off the tire, and then she was fine—but I was late to school. Ned McGraw saw me and said, 'You're late, and I know why.'

He told me that the woman had called the school. He knew that I had done the right thing."

Bob was friends with other politicians' sons, including Kevin Carey, the son of Governor Hugh Carey; Will Powers, whose father, Bill Powers, was the state Republican chairman; and Chris Scaringe, son of George Scaringe, who was the Albany County Republican chairman. "We [Kevin Carey and I] were good friends and I spent a lot of time at the mansion. It was quite an experience. We wanted to go to the same college." They did, graduating from Le Moyne in Syracuse. Howard said, "Bob really matured immensely at Le Moyne. He changed a lot."

Bob enjoyed working on his dad's campaigns. "It was fun, ringing doorbells and being around the campaign staff. We'd take trips down to Greene County and go to parades and fairs." But Bob realized that politics was not in his future. "I thought about politics. My father asked me after I graduated, but I didn't have the same passion for it. One of the things I didn't like in Albany was being in the spotlight. Everybody knew who I was. I like being *out* of the spotlight."

However, his own lack of interest in politics didn't deter Bob from appreciating his father's values: "I admire his will to help people. He's driven more than most people. He's one of the most determined people in the world. He's a very straight shooter. He always said, 'If you don't have something nice to say to someone, don't say anything.' He's lived that. I don't remember him saying negative things. Politics can be cutthroat. He lived with that."

Bob is married to Suzanne McDermott who is good friends with his sister Debbie. He and Suzanne have three children: the oldest son, Joe, graduated from Holy Cross. and crewed for them for four years. He now is employed by Franklin Templeton Investments in New York City. The second son,

Kevin, just graduated from the University of Scranton, where he was the starting catcher in baseball and majored in accounting. The third child, Kelly, will be a sophomore at Merrimack College in North Andover, Massachusetts."

Joe Nolan is grateful for the time he's spent with his grandfather. "I've always been close to him," Joe said. "I go to Saratoga with him every August. He made it a family thing"—just like Howard's dad did with Howard so many years ago.

Bob describes himself as a Democrat with "general Democratic philosophies. I'm always for the little guy. I look at my family. My family was very fortunate, but I want to see the same opportunities for people who can't afford it. Give people chances. That's the way my father's always been. I'm influenced by my father's work ethic and his desire to treat people right. That's what I was given by my father."

Howard's oldest child, fifty-seven-year-old Anne Davies, was born in the Naval Hospital at Camp Lejeune, North Carolina, in 1960. "Anne is very bright," Howard said. She attended Doane Stuart, a private high school in the south end of Albany that was founded in 1975. When Anne was sixteen, she and her siblings had to choose which parent they would live with, when Howard and Gerrie separated. Anne said, "My mother and I just didn't get along, so I decided to go with Dad. It was okay. We started traveling. I ended up in boarding school at Doane Stuart. I stayed there for about a semester of my junior year, but I would go home on the weekends."

By then, Anne had already worked on her dad's campaign ringing doorbells. "It was like, 'We're going away,'" she said. "I enjoyed it. It was fun the way we did it. One of us would go up to a house and say, 'My dad is running for the senate. Is it okay for him to stop by?' If they said no, we went on to the next house. I remember people would ask, 'Are you going to give me money if I vote for him?' That's what Albany politics was like. We campaigned hard. We'd start at seven o'clock in the morning and we'd be there the entire day. I did a lot of campaigning for my dad, almost five days a week. Somebody would pick me up at school."

Anne counted that as part of her interesting experience with her senator dad. "I got to spend a lot of time with my dad. We'd go to meetings, whatever. We traveled to Greene County, Cairo, every single fair. I'd feel bad for him. He'd be there to campaign and we'd be like, 'Dad, can we have some money?' with other people watching. It was a great racket." When she was sixteen, she attended the Governor's Ball with Howard. "It was really amazing," Anne said. "I'd be with him and he'd be talking to everyone. I learned things."

One thing Anne learned was that dining out with Howard could be a long process. "We couldn't walk into a restaurant without my dad stopping and saying hello to everyone. Then, as we ate, people came by our table. That's how it always was. He remembered people's names."

Anne relished the family get-togethers at Saratoga Race Course. "It was a lot of fun," she said. "Then we'd go to dinner afterward at Panza's on the lake or Century House or Wolferts Roost. We did eat well."

Considering that Howard won every time he ran for the state senate, election nights were a blast. "Always the same tradition," Anne said. "We'd all go out to dinner with the Aronowitzes and other couples. From there, we'd go to the hotel and watch the results. Reporters would be coming in and out. It was very exciting. We'd be there until twelve or one o'clock in the morning."

After high school, Anne worked briefly for the New York State Tax Department. "Then I was hired by New York Bell, which became NYNEX, then Bell Atlantic, and then it was Verizon. They gave us a cake every time we changed names." Anne began as a customer service rep, and then became a systems engineer and finally a senior account manager. "I got to travel, so it was fun."

On May 31, 2003, Anne's world turned upside down. Her only child, seventeen-year-old Christine, a straight-A student who had been riding horses since she was five, died in a riding accident at Krumkill Riding Stables in Bethlehem. She was taking jumping lessons with a friend when her horse caught his foot during a jump. Christine's foot came out of the stirrup and she fell off the horse. The horse fell on top of her.

"Christine was an incredible person," Anne said. "She was my best friend, and I was her best friend. A week before she died, she wrote all of these poems. She was only seventeen." Asked how she has coped with the tragedy, Anne said, "I struggle every day with it. Does it get easier? No, it becomes different."

Howard has struggled with it, too. "He was devastated," Anne said. "I have never seen him like that." Howard had spent a lot of time with Christine for an obvious reason. "My daughter just loved horses," Anne said. "She was over the top. Occasionally, he would pick her up at school and take her to Saratoga. She loved it." Howard said of Christine, "She was a lovely young lady."

Anne retired in 2006, and then went back to working for Verizon as a consultant in 2010. She continues to work for Currier McCabe Associates, which develops and supplies information technology services for human resource professionals. The president and CEO of the company, Kay Stafford, once worked for Howard at Delaware Plaza.

Kathy, Howard's second daughter, is fifty-six. At twelve

years of age, she overcame not only leukemia, but also a temporary paralysis from the waist down that had been caused by the experimental drugs that cured her leukemia. "Going through that stuff helps shape the person you become," she said. Kathy was in seventh grade when leukemia struck. "I was in the hospital for about two months in 1974, the same year my dad ran for the senate. l was in and out of school. In June, I wound up back in the hospital because I was paralyzed from the waist down. Eventually, I got feeling back in my lower legs, in my toes and upward."

Howard will forever remember the phone call. "I was in New York [City] at the time," he said. "I got a phone call early in the morning that Kathy had been diagnosed with leukemia, so I dashed back to Albany. She almost died for a long period, three months. Her doctor, Bill Sharfman, was best known for his work with leukemia patients. Over the years, he told me many times that he had never treated another person as sick as Kathy was who survived. It left her with stunted growth and a walking disability, but she survived. She has a lot of spunk, a lot of heart, and she's a very nice person."

Asked how she got through her ordeal, Kathy said, "My parents took me every step of the way—and my sisters and a close friend, Kathy Moran. You do what you have to do. Thankfully, everything went okay for me."

Her mom was one of the reasons. "My mom was there every day for me," Kathy said. "She'd get the kids off to school and come visit me every day, she or my aunt Judy. My mom was a wonderful woman. She was from Troy, went to Catholic High, and then got a full scholarship to Trinity College in Washington, DC, where she studied sociology. She did everything for her kids. We were number one in her eyes, especially when the grandkids came around. She was wonderful to them."

After graduating from the Academy of Holy Names, Kathy attended Siena College. She went to basketball games and got to know Kevin McGraw, a star guard whose dad, Ned, was the vice principal at Christian Brothers Academy.

Kathy first worked as an occupational therapy assistant for the Cerebral Palsy Center that Howard had cofounded. Then she worked for the New York State Office of General Services before beginning an eighteen-year tenure with New York State Senator Bill Stakowski from Buffalo, a good friend of Howard's who had starred in football at Holy Cross. "I enjoyed working there," Kathy said. "I worked with a wonderful woman, Millie Powers."

When Stakowski lost in a primary, Kathy was out of work for a year and a half before spending seven months working for Northway Toyota. She then got a job with the Albany County Department of Human Resources. She recently retired.

Kathy spent six years on the Upstate New York Board of Directors of the Leukemia and Lymphoma Society. "Somebody who was on the board asked me to get involved in one of their fund-raisers, so I said I was glad to. I wanted to do anything I could to help people not go through what I did and find a cure for this horrible disease."

Debbie Nolan Murray, fifty-five, Howard's third daughter, has carved out a unique niche in Howard's life. She works with him daily to manage the two shopping plazas he owns in Delmar, just south of Albany, and Plattsburgh, in upper northeastern New York. "We have a great working relationship," Debbie said.

That doesn't prevent Howard, who is in his Delmar office by seven thirty, from needling his daughter if she shows up fifteen minutes late. He'll greet her with "Good afternoon, Debbie." But they both can laugh at that. "We've always been close," Debbie said. "He's always been very involved in my life, and my other siblings would say the same. He was very engaging in conversation. He was always interested in what we did, how our day went, our outside activities. Always very positive, encouraging me. He made sure we'd go to events together as a family, like the Democratic picnic, the church bazaar, the fairs."

And, of course, they went to Saratoga Race Course. "Every Sunday was family day at the track," Debbie said. "As teenagers, that wasn't always our first choice, but we just did it. I swore I would never get in the horse business, and now I do all his horse stuff.

And there's the political stuff, too. "When he became a senator, I had a summer job helping out and stuffing envelopes at his office. I was fourteen, fifteen. By the time I went to college at Hartwick, my dad had numerous events in the evening. So he'd send me on his behalf, and I did a little bit of public speaking. That was very cool and good experience for me. I was like his liaison. It gave me a tremendous amount of confidence—the people we met, the encouragement. It gave me a sense of relating to people the way he does."

Debbie was a psychology major at Hartwick, but she took a job working for Key Bank in Albany. She has three children, Anthony, Kara, and Nicole—now thirty, twenty-seven, and twenty-three. Anthony graduated summa cum laude from Fordham University's School of Business and works in New York City in finance, Kara was cum laude at Siena College and is a fund-raiser for Holy Names Academy, and Nicole graduated from Providence College and has a marketing job in Boston. She's a computer whiz and an avid reader.

Debbie's second husband is Jim Murray, who has owned

the Murray Group, an insurance agency in Guilderland, for forty years. "He has three adult kids working for him," Debbie said.

Fifteen years ago, Debbie got a call from her dad. "My dad called me and said, 'Deb, come to the office. I want to talk to you.' So I drove over to Delmar, and he asked me, 'Is there any possibility that you want to run the family business?' He said it would be nice for someone else in the family to know the retail business."

Debbie wasn't working at the time, so she considered the offer. "As my kids got older, I was kind of getting antsy to do something. I actually thought of going to grad school. In the meantime, my dad was making changes in personnel at the office. All my other siblings had their careers and were working. My divorce was upcoming, but Dad told me, 'I know you have kids, so snow days are okay.' I could work on my hours, but have flexibility. The more I thought about it on my drive home, the more I thought I would do it."

Debbie started in January 2001. "It's been very interesting," she said. "Now it's full-time. It's intriguing. It's incredible to learn from my dad. He's been in the business for forty years. What I learned from him is valuable. You can take an irate tenant and show you understand. I pretty much run the show now. We work very well together. I remember him saying to me, 'Who's going to take better care of a business than a family member who's vested in it?' I think it gives him peace of mind to know that I'm just as committed to the property and the business as he is.

"My sister Karen and I were talking the other day," Debbie said. "We were remembering how we couldn't go out to dinner without somebody coming over to our table. Dad related so well to other people. It made us feel good. They'd say, 'Oh, my God, we love your father.'"

Howard's fourth daughter, Donna Nolan, now fifty-three, loved to go campaigning with her dad and siblings. "Every campaign was fun," she said, "and chaotic. I used to love going out. We had a good time together. It was exciting." Her favorite campaign story happened in Colonie. "We were campaigning, and this little old lady, who said she was very Republican, couldn't get her car started. She told Dad that if he got her car started, she'd vote for him." Howard got her car started. "I hope she was true to her word," Donna laughed, knowing that the only person who knew for sure was that little old lady.

Asked to explain her dad's success, Donna said, "I think he's very intelligent. He's very driven. He's very honest. And he really, really cares a lot for people. I remember a woman whose son was in prison. She went to see my dad in his office. She wanted him to talk to her son. Somewhere in the Newburgh area. He did it." Asked how she knew about it, Donna explained, "He canceled our plans to do something together that night."

Donna has worked for Verizon for thirty-two years. She works in the scheduling center for technicians "from Long Island to Buffalo, minus the five boroughs of New York City. I do enjoy my work."

Regarding Howard's relentless energy, she said, "It's healthy living for the most part. He's always very active, playing golf and tennis. He played sports since a young age. He never smoked a cigarette. He was in the marines. And he has a love for life."

Lynn Nolan Hyde, fifty, Howard's fifth daughter, spent one year at Niagara University and then, after a bad case of homesickness, finished her studies at Hudson Valley Community College. A friend of hers got her a job at Key Bank and Lynn worked her way up, landing a job with Fleet

Bank, which was bought out by Bank of America, where she works today as a systems programmer. "I love it," she said. "I troubleshoot problems. I get to do new things. My mind is always going, and that's what I love." She's been working from home in East Greenbush full-time since 2005. "I'm very focused. I'm on call 24/7/365."

Lynn cherishes her childhood memories. "There were seven of us. Our next-door neighbor had a huge yard where we used to play kickball and baseball. We'd sleigh-ride down their yard into a big field. I remember playing football. It was great to have six siblings. We hung out and did everything together."

Lynn describes her father as "a go-getter" who "wanted to do something with his life. So he took the bull by the horns and he did it. He knows how to talk to people. He was one of those who was there for his constituents. He was there for his people. It was never about himself. He has a heart of gold. I still get introduced as Howard Nolan's daughter, which makes me feel great. He is still respected in the community."

Now divorced, Lynn has two daughters–Paige, twenty-two, and Ashley, twenty. Paige graduated from Le Moyne College with a bachelor of science degree in physics and math. She has work experience in the environmental field involving asbestos removal. A talented artist, Ashley is studying mortuary science at Hudson Valley Community College.

Since Shannon was out of town, Lynn was Howard's date when the Knickerbocker Arena—the civic center in downtown Albany, now the Times Union Center—opened its doors with a concert by Frank Sinatra.

Lynn is thankful that her dad has Shannon in his life. "My dad found Shannon and was as happy as a man can be—and he still is." However, Lynn had trouble dealing with her parents' separation and ultimate divorce. "It was hard. I was number six of seven children. The older ones were like, 'It's time.' I was the emotional one in the family, so it was tough. I don't think my mother ever got over him. She was Catholic. You only get married once. She had a heart of gold. She would give the shirt off her back to anyone."

Shortly after she visited her mother for the last time, Gerrie Leonard died on January 2, 2016, at the age of seventy-eight. "I still cry every day," Lynn said.

At forty-nine, Karen Nolan Cummings is the youngest Nolan child. A graduate of Niagara University, Karen went into the banking industry, first with Fleet Bank, which became Bank of America, and then part-time for Met Life. She has now joined the family business, replacing her niece Kara (Debbie's daughter), who had been working as bookkeeper. Karen has two children, Nolan, thirteen and Lauryn, ten. Karen is married to Rob Cummings, a dentist. Her son, Nolan, who goes to St. Gregory's School, is a star athlete in basketball and a member of the swim team at Schuyler Meadows Country Club, where he also enjoys playing golf. Lauryn, also at St. Gregory's, loves to read, like her mother, and has artistic talent.

Though she didn't spend a lot of time with her busy dad, Karen said, "When we were together, it was quality time. Every time we went somewhere—museums, Broadway shows in New York—it might not have been a ton of time, but it was fun." She also enjoyed working on her dad's campaigns until she started college.

Asked if she's proud of her dad's success in politics, Karen said, "Of course. He was very charismatic. He's a very kind, nice person. Any time we'd go out to dinner, it would take a half hour to get out because he'd stop and visit people. It was like a running joke: 'Here he goes again.' He wouldn't just say hello—he'd engage in conversation. And he didn't do it because he had to; he did it because he loved to. Even in Florida by the pool, he wouldn't lie down. He'd be out talking to people all around the pool. He seemed to know people everywhere we went, even once in Paris fifteen years ago. He just never stopped."

He still hasn't.

Chapter 20

STILL GOING

After marking his eighty-fifth birthday in August 2017, Howard is realistic—and appreciative. "My whole starting football team from CBA is dead," he said. "Both senior partners in my law firm, Mark Heller and Richard Weiner, and my business partner, Mac MacFarland, are all dead. I've been very, very fortunate health-wise."

He was never more fortunate than nine years ago, when he couldn't keep up with Shannon on a Thursday morning walk in Boynton Beach, their Florida home before they relocated to Fort Lauderdale in 2011. "Shannon and I used to walk five times a week," Howard said. "We hadn't gone four blocks or so when I got a pain in my shoulder and it went down my leg. I stopped to almost a crawl. She thought I should go to the doctor." In fact, Shannon insisted that he act immediately.

They were scheduled to fly back to Albany the following week, and Howard initially said he'd wait until then to make an appointment and get it checked out. But when Howard took a stroll to buy a newspaper that afternoon, Shannon took advantage of his absence to call Howard's general practitioner. Dr. James Puleo Sr. had followed Howard by two years at Christian Brothers Academy and had been a basketball star at Manhattan College. Puleo told Shannon that he wanted to see Howard immediately, and then he called Howard and told him to come to his office Monday morning in Albany.

Howard called his cousin Tom, who once had to have stents in his heart, and Tom agreed that Howard should see his doctor immediately. So Howard saw Dr. Puleo that Monday and took a stress test on Tuesday. Three days later, he underwent a triple bypass. "I've got to give Shannon credit for saving my life," Howard said. "She's wonderful, absolutely wonderful."

His heart has been fine since the operation, but Howard received a diagnosis of prostate cancer in 2014. He was treated with radiation "twelve weeks, five days a week," Howard said. "When it was all finished, they did another test and it was a perfect result."

Then an old minor problem became more serious in 2016. "Fifteen or sixteen years ago, a doctor discovered an aneurysm on my aorta," Howard said. "They told me that if it didn't get bigger, it's not a problem. I had it checked every year, and it was always the same—until last year, when it was a little bigger. This year, a lot bigger. I was urged to take care of it because if it ruptures …" Doctors put a stent in Howard's aorta in April 2017. "So far, so good," he said. "They'll keep taking pictures every four months or so, then every six months, then once a year."

Howard also had to deal with skin cancer in 2017. A dermatologist found three sites, and Howard had three surgeries—one on his nose, a second on his left sideburn around his ear, and the third on his chest.

So, though it was personally painful to do, Howard scaled back on his work schedule, but only to a point. Even the idea of missing work upsets him. "From the day I started practicing law until I retired from law, I missed one day of work for a hernia [the famous hernia]," Howard said. "I was back in the office the next day, although I was a little sore."

Now he knows that he can't be there every day. "My life is tapering down to where I have to decide how to spend my time and what I'm capable of doing in terms of work," he said. When he's in Albany, he'll sometimes show up at his Delaware Plaza office at seven thirty in the morning. And he'll still make long, six-hour trips to his plaza in Plattsburgh and back.

Much of Howard's plaza business is now handled ably by his daughters Debbie and Karen. "Debbie, and now my daughter Karen, both are very capable. Most of the business has shifted to them, and they are quite good at that. They're smart and quick learners, and they've done a great job."

With less work to do, Howard has enjoyed his life more. He still reads six or seven newspapers daily, a book a week, and four or five magazines a month. But he doesn't use a computer, and he has no personal e-mail. His love of horses lives on, and it doesn't require work to enjoy the highlights. Howard knows they can't all be stars, a lesson he learned decades ago.

Howard still loves to travel. In early June, he and Shannon spent five days in Las Vegas. "In the last few years, I've spent on the average eight months a year away from New York," he said. "We traveled a lot. Every year, once or twice to San Francisco, to Las Vegas primarily to go to shows, France every year, Italy close to once a year. We went to Spain. And we used to go six times a year for a week or two each time in Argentina. Some of the grandchildren visited us down there and in France as graduation gifts."

Howard couldn't be happier than to spend this quality

time with Shannon, whom he still adores. "We just have a wonderful life, and I can't say enough nice things about her. She's smart. She's pretty. She's energetic, and a very good tennis player. She won championships at Coral Ridge Country Club."

Shannon has loved the adventure of spending her life with Howard. "When I met Howard, it was magical," she said. "It was a lot of fun for me. He was a big shot in Albany. I met some wonderful people. We went to interesting places. We were a blessed couple, because he was successful and I had free travel. We had the advantage that other couples didn't have." Their biggest advantage was being the right person for each other.

Howard was the right person for his Albany constituents, too. "It's funny, but still to this day, no matter where I go out with him, someone knows the man," Howard's daughter Lynn said. "People remember him and he is respected." He's earned it.

INDEX

194

H

Harriman, Averill 53
Head, Alec 152
Head, Criquette 152
Heller, Julius 16, 22
Heller, Justin vii, 87
Heller, Mark 3, 22, 45, 46, 54, 67,
    87, 92, 105, 189
Hickey, Carmela 50
Hickey, Michael 50
Hicks, Elizabeth "Tish" 75
Hicks, John vii, 74
Hines, Sonny 142
Hirsch, Joe 142
Hoblock, Michael 166
Holden, Father Edgar 22
Hough, Stan 127
Howe, Peter 163
Hubbard, Bishop Howard 160
Hyde, Lynn Nolan 185

I

India Halo 173
Instrument Landing 127
Irish Colonial 34, 169, 170
Irish River 140
Irish Whisper 76

J

Java Gold 139
Jennings, Jerry vii, 4, 73, 142, 156
Jensen, Barbara 131, 159
Johnson, Karen 168
Johnson, Lyndon 54
Joyce, Harold 119

K

Kahn, Larry 68

Karen's Lady 121
Keating, Ken 52
Kelso 163
Kennedy, Ted 3, 32, 51
King, Larry vii, 5, 131, 155
Kinum, John 67
Klein, Calvin 104
Klein, Rayfield "Rafie" 48
Koch, Ed 112
Koehler, Monique vii, 161
Krone, Julie 142, 169
Krulak, Victor 48

L

Langan, Kevin 60, 95, 138
Langan, Mary 60
Langley, Walter 66, 67
LaRouche, John 29
Layne, Bobby 11
LeBrun, Fred 23
Lehman, Herbert 12
Lindsay, John 93
Lodge, Henry Cabot 51
Logan, Henry Clayton 97
Logan, Marcia (Goodgame) 62, 98
Logan, Mary 62, 98
Logan, Ruth McAuley 98
Luddy, Bob 43
Lukas, D. Wayne 139
Luro, Horatio 26

M

MacFarland, Norris "Mac" 46,
    47, 189
MacFarland, Peggy vii
Mack, Earl 146
Magnier, Paul 138
Magovern, Malcolm 36
Malloy, Charlie 32

O'Sullivan, Ray 11

P

Palermo, Pat vii, 5, 105
Panner II, Edward 111
Pardue, Homer 34
Pataki, George 94, 167
Patrick, Jim 122
Penna, Elinor 163
Perkins, Homer 89
Peterson, James Hardin 97
Picchi, Joe 77
Pikulski, Diana vii, 163
Piscarelli, Bob 37
Plus Value 138
Powers, Bill 177
Powers, Millie 182
Powers, Will 177
Prentiss, Bob 109
PR Man 126
Promised Road 164
Proskin, Arnold 81, 94
Pucek, John 124
Puleo Sr., Dr. James 189

Q

Quick Card 124, 125

R

Rampling, Charlotte 99
Read the Footnotes 170
Readtheprospectus 170
Regal Embrace 125, 126
Regan, Edward "Ned" 94, 176, 182
Reinfurt, Ed vii, 74
Rico Monte 26
Ritvo, Tim 173
Roberts, Ron 22

Rockne, Knute 32
Rodeo 127
Rohatyn, Felix 96
Roman, Joyce vii, 45, 160
Roosevelt, Franklin Delano 12
A Rose for Shannon 169
Royal Value 138, 139
Rutnik, Doug 81
Ryan, Jimmy 68, 78, 85
Ryan, Matt 53

S

Sagace 140, 150
Sanseverino, Ralph 125
Santos, Jose ii, 169
Sauque, Frederick 138, 140, 141, 142
Scaringe, Chris 177
Scaringe, George 177
Schoenborn, Gus 127
Schulhofer, Scotty 169
Secretariat 137, 163
Shapoff, Skippy 163
Shaw, George Bernard 161
Sheehan, James 113
Signoracci, Robert 156
Sinatra, Frank 147, 186
Slutzky, Orville 49
Smith, Al 12
Smith, Tom 121, 123, 124
Spath, Tom 22
Spend A Buck 123
Spotlight 47
Stafford, Kay 180
Stakowski, Bill 182
Stallone, Sylvester 99
Stronach, Frank 173
Stuart, Mark 118
Sutton, Percy 93

Sweeney, Mike 55

T

Talon 26
Taylor, E. P. 125
Teabout, Nona 131, 159
Thomas, Helen 100
Thomas, Joe 126
Tiller 125
Times Union 4, 23, 50, 77, 82, 83,
    85, 88, 94, 95, 109, 110, 111,
    114, 118, 134, 154, 155, 156,
    157, 186
Tishmeister 76
Toomey, William 29
Top Command 137
Touhey, Carl 70, 77, 79
Tracy, Mary 107
Treadway, Ann 47
Tremper, Jim 164
Tweed, Boss 4

V

Van Buren, Martin 49
Veitch, John 149
Verne, Jules 16, 96

Victoria Park 126
Vitello, Paul 82
Vowinkel, John "Rip" 17, 18

W

Walker, Jimmy 12
Wallingford, Dr. 34
War Hero 10, 117
Warsh, Bob vii, 24
Weiner, Rich 44
Weingarten, Gene 79
Weiss, Leonard 68, 74, 156, 157
Werblin, Sonny 126
Whalen, Tom 44, 144
Wildenstein, Daniel 138, 151
Williams, Dwayne 131, 159
Willkie, Wendell 12
Wilson, Malcolm 79

Y

Young, Father Peter 129
Yunich, David 126

Z

Zwack, Barbara (Ardman) 159